Freesourcing

How to Start a Business with No Money

Jonathan Yates

CAPSTONE

This edition first published 2009

Registered office

Capstone Publishing Ltd. (A Wiley Company), The Atrium, Southern Gate, Chichester, West Sussex, PO19 8SQ, United Kingdom

For details of our global editorial offices, for customer services and for information about how to apply for permission to reuse the copyright material in this book please see our website at www.wiley.com.

Library of Congress Cataloguing-in-Publication Data

9781906465803

A catalogue record for this book is available from the British Library.

Set in 11.5 on 14 pt Calibri by Toppan Best-set Premedia Limited

Printed in Great Britain by TJ International Ltd, Padstow, Cornwall

Contents

Introduction vii
About This Book xi

1 Use What You Have 1
   Time 2
   Family, friends and your social network 6
   What's lying around? 15
   Creativity 19
   Emotion 23
   The art of barter 25
   Experience 28
   Prices and negotiation 31
   The entrepreneurial advantage 33

2 Setting Up the Foundations of Your
   Business 37
   Elevator pitch 38
   The legal entity 42
   Using professional help 43
   Business plan 44
   A place to work 47
   Money 51
   Travel 57
   Sourcing equipment 59
   Food for thought 64
   Business cards 65
   Making yourself look bigger than you are 66
   Protecting your ideas 68
   Trial business services 72
   Banking 73

3 IT and Communication 77
   Computer equipment 79
   Getting on the Internet 84
   Data storage and back-up 87
   Email and website 89
   Communication 95
   Webinars 101
   Template documentation 103
   Professional business applications 104

4 Help, Skills and Training — 111
Ask for help — 112
Get new skills — 114
Community skill sharing — 117
Find a mentor — 119
Motivate yourself — 122

5 Research, Innovation and Prototypes — 125
Research — 125
Generate great ideas — 132
Sell what you have — 133
Get money to turn ideas into products — 137
Start a business-to-business software company — 138
White labelling — 140
Getting stocked up — 143

6 Customers, Brands, Marketing and Sales — 151
Create your own brand — 152
Find customers — 154
Get publicity — 162
Obtain testimonials — 170
Read trade magazines — 171
Benefit from an army of sales people — 174
Get accredited — 177
Attend exhibitions — 179
Get paid in advance — 182

7 Growth and Next Steps — 189
Forms of growth capital — 191
Some inspiration — 193

Freestarts: More Businesses You Can Start for Free — 199
The 10 Rules of Freesourcing — 217

Glossary — 220
Acknowledgements — 222
About the Author — 223

Introduction

You've had the big idea—well done! It's taken absolutely ages to knock your epiphany into shape, but you're sure this is the big one. Your current product development team—you, your mates, that shopping trip to the supermarket and the Internet research you did the other night at 2 a.m.—have been honing the business model down the pub for nearly two weeks and quite frankly, you can't believe it hasn't been done already. It's so simple that someone else must have surely seen the opportunity? No, according to the Internet and the supermarket, you are the only one with this money-making idea that will change the way the world turns. It's time to take the next step...but I bet you don't.

You see, this is where the majority of business ideas stop. What a shame, what a waste and what a missed opportunity! Never mind, at least you can talk about what might have been and when someone mentions to you the new multimillion-pound concept that's in the newspapers, you can always say you had the idea first. Then back to the pub for some creative idea generation.

The main problem seems to be motivation to spend your own money on getting the idea to the next stage. Inevitably you will question yourself and the idea: what if it fails, what will my development team think if everything goes pear shaped? And the classic excuse: I have no money to start a business.

This is where *Freesourcing* comes in. You don't need your own money to start your business. What? Yes, that's right, you can start a business right now with those two little friends I often call on, time and effort.

There's an entire industry dedicated to helping you take your idea and do something with it. The secret is—and not many people get this bit, so hang on in there, as it's a bit complicated—the secret is that entrepreneurship and innovation are the wheels that grease the entire UK economy and keep Britain Great. The government pulls out all the stops to help people with ideas translate them into start-ups and then into profitable businesses. It's in the UK's interest for you to make your idea happen; more than that, it's your *responsibility* to make it happen. So what are you waiting for? Money?

Freesourcing is a definitive guide for free business start-up resources (freesources, geddit?). I will show you where to look for free help to start up your business and get it to a point where you can earn an income and take the idea to the growth stage on your own.

Freesourcers not only think outside the box, they wonder where they can get a box for free.

Large empty cardboard box—Would this be of any use to someone moving house? 27" high × 16" × 16". Collection from XXX. Will discard after today if no replies. Cheers XXXXXX—from www.freecycle.org

Freesourcing covers free premises, free money, free computers, free legal help, free banking, free networking, free stock. In fact, apart from this book, which at £9.99 is a snip, you could build your empire with £0.

About This Book

This book is intended to help you start your business for free using the ideas, enthusiasm and resources that you already have at your disposal. The stuff lying around your house, your social network, your emotion and drive—all the things you have amassed in your life so far can be put to good use in helping you create a profitable and growing business venture. Do you really need money to make money or can you start for free on your quest for financial freedom? That is the aim of this book, the freesourcing quest for freedom.

What kind of business do you want to start? Are you looking to change the world or are you happy with just running a business that enables you to take control of your life? Is the business you intend to start going to take five days to get going or five years? This book covers all sorts of business empires—what they have in common is that they generate an income and are started with no money whatsoever.

Freesourcing is an ethic, an idea and a plan to create something from nothing. In a way, it means you have to regress to childhood and search out your creativity to enjoy using simple and free solutions to get your idea off the ground. People from all over the world have started businesses for free in a multitude of ways and I would like to share with you some of their strategies.

Most of the ideas in this book are free. What does free mean? Free means that a product or service is provided without, or is not subject to, a charge or payment. Free means not having to pay cash for something you need in your business. I stress the phrase "not having to pay cash", because the freesourcer may have to pay in time or in kind where appropriate.

In the UK television programme *The Apprentice*, Sir Alan Sugar is always going on about minimizing costs. His success can be attributed to a keen eye for an opportunity and embracing cost savings and efficiencies at the most fundamental level of his business empire. This is part of the *Freesourcing* ethic. Most companies do this when they've been trading for a while: they turn the looking glass back on themselves and ask where they can be more efficient. In this book I suggest that you should start out like this and use freesourcing to grow. This is what an entrepreneur does.

> *Entrepreneurs are people who spend a few years of their life like some people won't, the rest of their lives like some people can't.*

Be aware of the fact that there will always be some things you are unable to freesource. Each business start-up is different and there is no set process. The best advice when faced with something you need to pay for is to find a viable free alternative or find a way around it. Minimize cost at all junctions in the process—in other words, become an entrepreneur.

The word entrepreneur is used all over the media and is a catch-all term for anyone starting their own business, whatever the size.

Here are some widely recognized descriptions of entrepreneurs (taken from *100 All-Time Essentials for Entrepreneurs* by Jonathan Yates, so giving me a free plug!). Which one are you?

→ *Altrepreneur*—Looks for a change of lifestyle and not just increased wealth. Their motivations are not for financial reward but a change of circumstances.
→ *Mompreneur*—Parents who stay at home and use the time between looking after and raising their children to begin and grow a business from home.
→ *Wantrapreneur*—A person who would like to start a business and is actively engaged in finding the right starting point.
→ *Entrepreneur*—An entrepreneur makes money out of ever-changing market opportunities fuelled by the enjoyment of making a profit.
→ *Solopreneur*—Individual entrepreneurs, in business for themselves, motivated by money and achievement and success on their own merit.
→ *Ultrapreneur* (or serial entrepreneur)—Someone who actively reinvests their money into ever larger business ventures, not solely for the financial gain but also for the enjoyment of the process.
→ *Freesource(u)r*—An entrepreneur who has started and grown their business with no money apart from that which the company has generated.

There is a certain amount of celebrity status associated with entrepreneurs and you get maximum credibility points if you can say you have started out on your own. But don't just use the word, know what it really means. This book will help you understand one of the facets of being an entrepreneur, namely that you need to see an opportunity and take advantage of it, maximizing revenues and minimizing costs, which is the essence of keeping start-up costs to a minimum.

When using freesources, you might expect there to be a lack of quality. It does hold true that if you demand quality in a timely manner you need to pay for it, otherwise the benefits of a competitive capitalist business environment would not work. However, free does not always mean quality so strive to find quality freesources where you can.

You will notice as you read this book that each section ends with a Freeq statement. Freeq is the freesourcing equivalent quotient. It's a mark of how much cash you will be saving by following the advice. Where possible, I have given a cash value that directly correlates to your saving. When this is not possible, I have used a time comparator for the free-source instead. However, in both cases remember that the Freeqs should not be taken as exact values but as a mark of where you should be looking to gain savings. The Freeqs I have chosen represent costs at the high end of the scale and better value may be achieved by shopping around.

As well as no-cost options, I have provided some excellent value low-cost options for you to have a look at as viable alternatives. And, if you're stuck for ideas of what business

to start, you'll find many Freestart suggestions for businesses you can begin for free throughout the book, and
particularly in Chapter 8.

How are you going to start *your* business for free?

1

Use What You Have

So you have an idea for a business, which is brilliant. I am truly very excited for you, as this is the moment when your creativity knows no bounds. This is when your senses are most heightened and the constraints on what you can do have not yet reared their difficult and ugly heads.

This is the moment the pathway starts to unfold in front of you and you can map out your future. Grasp this moment and ride the wave of creativity for as long as possible, learning and understanding what it means to be an entrepreneur on the way. This is your moment to use what you have to make it happen. Don't leave that great idea lying on the table for another second, or it may slip away for ever.

In this chapter you will find out how to open your eyes and see what you have available to you immediately. It's Day 1 and you have decided to take your idea forward. There are specific fundamentals that you must get your hands on to move one square at a time over the snakes and ladders board of your entrepreneurial journey.

The most appropriate way to begin is to collect together everything you have available to you right now. Look around the house, in your attic and in the garage and see what you already have. Take the opportunity to reappraise those things you've been meaning to throw away and see them in a new light, reflecting the creativity of your new idea. They may be bits of junk now, but how could they benefit your business? The same goes for everything in your life: friends, family, experiences, money and, most importantly, you.

The trick is to think creatively about your life so far, the experiences you have gained and the people you know. This is your starting point, so use what you have.

Time

Time is the greatest, most widely available and least expensive freesource you have at your immediate disposal.

You need to understand straight away that 100% of freesourcing has an actual cost. That cost is your time and a whole load of effort. You have to make adjustments to your life in order to create the time you need to start and grow your business. This is a simple but essential step.

You often hear the saying that time is not money, but actually it's not. Time is a measurement of our progress through the universe, whereas money is a system of exchange. You need to view the link between time and money as a system of exchange with which to barter new assets to grow your business.

But do you have any spare time? Think back to the last time someone said they were too busy or there aren't enough hours in the day. It wasn't that long ago, was it? I bet you've said something similar in the last week or so.

There are 24 hours in a day and 60 minutes in an hour, which is 1440 minutes every day. What are you doing right this minute, right now, to benefit yourself? (I know, reading this book!) You should be asking yourself this question every minute of every day: What could I be doing in my freetime?

Here's a test for you. What do you do with your 24 hours each day?

Note in the list below how much time you usually allocate to each activity:

Getting up
Breakfast
Lunch
Dinner
Travel
Work
Chores
Watching TV
Socializing
Sleeping

What could you be doing with your day instead? There's a difference between existing and living. Search out the spare minutes in your day and group them together to create a space for you to get something meaningful done.

What do you do with the time between your usual activities? What's the first thing you do when you wake up? Make a conscious effort to be prepared for the day ahead, but do it the night before and prepare yourself for those things that will make this a "doing" day. Set your alarm 15 minutes earlier—it's only 15 minutes' less sleep, after all, but it could make all the difference.

What about when you're travelling to and from work? Do you listen to a podcast on recent industry trends or do you read the free newspaper, then catch up on some sleep because you got up late again?

Do two things at once: go for a run to clear your head, get a bit fitter and listen to something useful on your MP3 player. Read trade magazines and always have the news on in the background. Learn to be creative with your time and let it work for you instead of continually chasing after it. Manage your time so you can do what's important to you with an ongoing and ever-changing plan.

How do you make your time work for you? Organize your life simply by using lists, create efficient systems for doing things, set aside time for the difficult jobs and don't just do the easy ones. Do the things you enjoy doing first to motivate yourself to do more.

We all get caught up in the difficulties of life and spread our time thinly by committing to coaching the junior rugby section or tidying up the garden. Apply some rationality and set aside the time you need to get your business running. Go to bed early and get up early—change your lifestyle to enable you to commit more time to getting your business running effectively. And remember always to spend quality time with your family, as they are your second greatest asset when starting a business.

Time is one thing you can trade freely because it's yours, you are in control. You get to decide where you are going to be and what you are going to do while you're there. You may not have any cash to buy goods and services, but you do have time.

People have been bartering time and effort for goods and services for eons, so revitalize those skills. Think about the cliché for what happens when you're in a restaurant and you discover you've left your wallet at home: when the bill arrives, you start negotiating how much washing up you have to do before you can go home. This works for your business too.

To get the business moving, offer to work in a local shop for a morning and instead of the proprietor paying you any money, ask for something tangible that you need in return. Buy an axe so that you can go out to the local woods, take the free wood on offer from the council and chop it into kindling to sell on at £2 a bag. You could take the money you make and add it to your logo design fund or buy some more materials. Be creative in what you ask for, work hard and ensure good value for your time.

Get busy working on the things that matter and make a difference to the growth of your business right now!

 Professional time management course, 1 day at **£375**.

Family, friends and your social network

Apart from you, your time and your amazing idea, the next greatest asset you have is your network.

Your family will always help where they can: they are unselfish and would always like to help you become a success in whatever you decide to undertake. Unfortunately, this act of selflessness in itself can be a hindrance, as they want you to succeed so much that they always think encouragement is the best advice, when perhaps from time to time you really need them to say no to one of your ideas.

Ask your family for financial help when you need it, and for assistance with getting your hands on the kit you have to have to carry out your business. Ask them as well for access to contacts and possible sales leads. And go to your family when you're overworked and need a helping hand fulfilling a big order.

As a next step, you should increase your business "family" by extending the reach of your business and social networks.

People do business with other people. If you grow your network, you have more people to do business with.

Your social network is everyone you have ever spoken to, emailed, posted to in a forum, answered on Twitter, went to school with or done business with. It includes Glen down the pub, Barry, Stephanie and Paul who are parents at the kids' school, and not forgetting Janet the babysitter. You get the idea: your social network is everyone and anyone you can refer to for advice because you have a history with them in one form or another.

Strangers are friends you have yet to meet.

A social network is a structure. The structure is made up of a collection of points that are connected by intersections such as values, visions, ideas, exchange, friendship and so on. In the real world this will be your network of friends, your family, customers and suppliers, investors and any club affiliations you may have. The key factor is that you all have something in common. In many instances, the thing you have in common is other people.

But a time will come when your current network has been exhausted and you have to explore new opportunities to grow the business. This is when you need to spend some time expanding both your business and social networks. There are numerous business networking clubs that may charge a joining fee so you can be part of their group. These clubs are great if you want to get to know a particular group of people well, but unless you're joining as part of an active recruitment drive, you won't necessarily be meeting many new people. Instead, I would look for casual groups of like-minded people who meet on a regular basis and can act both as support for your growing business and as an extended sales force who can recommend your products and services.

When I had a problem with hand packing an order for a large contract, I went to a mate at the squash club and asked whether I could use one of the courts as a manufacturing room, if they were not too busy. He asked the managers and then, although I had not asked for assistance, offered his and his friends' services for the entire weekend to come and help me out. The job was to create 5000 packs of goodies, take a silver envelope, put in a product and a flyer, close the envelope, add a sticker and put the envelope in a box. Although this doesn't sound a lot, it takes a long time. Thanks to my free help, we finished 30 hours later and I was able to post the job to the customer on Monday, a day earlier than she had wanted. I bought my 10 helpers lunch in the form of 3 tons of pizza, which did cost me money, but the return on the contract was a lot more than £50. Thank you Harrogate Squash and Fitness.

The idea of a social network translates very well into the virtual world of the Internet, where you can find very large groups of like-minded people connected by their interests and their connections to other people. Whatever area your business is in, there will be someone out there who can help you understand more about your chosen topic. You just have to find them.

The following are some of the tools that can be used to connect to and grow your social network:

→ Audioboo, http://audioboo.fm
→ Blogger, http://www.blogger.com
→ Facebook, http://www.facebook.com
→ Friendfeed, http://friendfeed.com
→ iPadio, http://www.ipadio.com
→ LinkedIn, http://www.linkedin.com
→ MySpace, http://www.myspace.com
→ Ning, http://www.ning.com
→ Twitter, http://twitter.com
→ Wordpress, http://wordpress.org
→ Xing, http://www.xing.com
→ YouTube, http://www.youtube.com

There are many more sites popping up every day, but these are established and my own personal picks.

Recently LinkedIn, Facebook and Twitter have become the tools of choice for business start-ups, so to help you get started there's a little more on each of these below, together with the newcomer Audioboo.

LinkedIn

LinkedIn (www.linkedin.com) provides solid business net-working. It acts as a central database connecting individual professionals together to share ideas, information and opportunities. There are currently around 40 million people actively registered on the site.

The main idea is that you create a profile and ask people you know well to link to you. When they link to you, you can see who they are connected to. They may be connected to someone you want to do business with, and if so you can ask for an introduction to this person through your initial LinkedIn contact. Simple. Now multiply this by 20 primary LinkedIn connections. That's 20 people you know really well with anything between 10 and 1000 connections of their own. Can you see the power of this networking tool?

As a free tool, LinkedIn goes even further. You can search for people by company. In this search, you don't even have to know who the people are, just which company you would like to do business with. The search will bring up all the people who work or who have worked for this company and are linked via your network, as well as how you can approach them. There's even more! In order to contact anyone from a search freely, join a LinkedIn group particular to your business type (go to www.linkedin.com/groups to explore what's available). When you next search for a contact, the first results will be those people who have joined the same group. The example here explains more.

I would like to introduce my new product to UK super-markets, but have no idea who to contact. I could cold call and ask to speak to the widget buyer at a UK retailer, then introduce myself. That's the traditional way. With LinkedIn I join the UK retail industry professionals group. I then search for the buyer in a particular company. I find, luckily, that she is in the same UK retail industry professional group, as is her boss and some of the people she works with. The search also brings up people who have previously worked with the company, one of whom I met by chance at an exhibition recently and is on my LinkedIn network already. I can contact the buyer with an email directly from LinkedIn and mention that I met the ex-colleague at a show and they liked the product and suggested I get in touch.

So as free services go, LinkedIn hits the nail squarely on the head.

facebook

"Facebook helps you connect and share with the people in your life." (from www.facebook.com)

Facebook has many benefits as a freesource. Mostly used by friends and families, it's a great way to hook back up with old friends and get to know what they're up to. You already have some history with these people from your past, so reacquaint yourselves and get to know how you might be able to help them and how they might be able to help you out as well. Those brothers in the year below you at school might well be property millionaires by now, so if they can help you, get back in touch.

You can set up a Facebook group to create a buzz around your business. If you have a new product to sell, start a Facebook group, get your friends to join and do a great deal for them if they buy direct from you. They might just buy the product out of interest to see what you're up to, they might like the product and tell their friends, who might also buy the product. People are nosy and they love to know what you've been up to, so tell them!

You can see my Facebook profile at www.facebook.com/jonyates and, once you've joined, explore Facebook groups at www.facebook.com/grouphome.php.

Twitter

Twitter (www.twitter.com) helps you keep in touch with people who are interested in following what you're up to. It's a "microblogging" tool, which enables you to post information to a website or network in a concise form rather than the traditional endless reams of info in more established, unlimited blogs. The Twitter form of microblogging limits what you have to say to a mere 140 characters, which focuses your attention on what information you actually need to convey to make your post valuable. Of course, you have to gain followers, people who have consciously made the effort to follow your messages, but you can do this by handing out your Twitter username at every opportunity: on emails, on your business card and so on. Once you have a set of followers, you can inform them of the goods and services you offer.

Let's have a look at an example.

Chris has a photographic studio. He started in true free-source style with no cash and has built his business to the point where he has 40 clients who follow him on Twitter. His family and friends also follow him, so he has a grand total of 91 followers.

Things have been a bit slow for Chris's business, so he sends out a tweet (in 140 characters or fewer, as is the rule with Twitter):

20 family photos 20 mins for £20 sat 8th May, South Park Studios, Wimbledon 09:30 first 20 get a free framed print.

Let's say that five people from Chris's 91-person network think this is a good idea. They copy this message and send it on to their own extended networks. For the sake of this example, each network has 100 people in it, so now another 300 have seen the message about the special offer. Three people from each of these networks send it to their network, and so on. The message could bring in a lot of people on the day, if they are close to the studio and if they want a family portrait. Twitter can help you to get in touch with a whole new customer base for free, very quickly and efficiently.

I have used Twitter for a while now, not only to sell my books and professional speaking services, but also to keep people informed about our retail products and to stay in touch with how competitors do things. I have Twitter search on my name, my book titles and my brands, so that whenever someone mentions any of these I am notified by email and can respond. For the first time in history, customers and suppliers can have real-time, direct feedback on specific products and services. This is a great marketing opportunity and offers brilliant possibilities for boosting customer service.

If you want to follow me on Twitter, here are my contact details: www.twitter.com/jonathanyates and www.twitter.com/freesources.

Audioboo

Audioboo (http://audioboo.fm) is to podcasting as Twitter is to microblogging. Audioboo is an application for the iPhone that you can use to record a short, thought-provoking snippet on whatever subject you wish to inform the world about. You can automatically upload this "boo" to your Audioboo account and it is there for all the world to listen to.

I link my Audioboo account to Twitter so that as soon as I post a new boo, it is blogged onto the Twitter network and anyone who's following me can hear what I have to say.

There's a service at http://ping.fm that allows you to update many of these networking sites at once, instead of having to log into each individually, update your status and then do the same thing again with the next one. Ping.fm sends an update to all your feeds with the same message in a single hit.

Social networking tools can also be used to monitor your brands, personal name, business suppliers and competitors. All you need to do is to save a search on Twitter and other sites that alert you when particular keywords are triggered. For example, I have an account set up at notify.me (http://notify.me) that emails me whenever my name, my books or my brands are mentioned in blog posts, picture uploads, news feeds or any other form of information held on the Internet. It has proved very useful indeed. I have also come across a whole new section of the world populated by other people with the same name!

A word of warning: be diligent with security. Criminals will pay good money to get their hands on your online identity and identity theft is on the increase. The more people know about you, the more business you can conduct with them— but at the same time, the more people know about you, the more business they can conduct without you!

There are many ways of creating a healthy networking environment around you that can provide free solutions to your everyday business problems in a fraction of the time it would have taken by traditional means. Rather than banging your head against a brick wall, just ask for help!

freeq A single networking event lasting a full day can cost **£350** to meet between 2 and 30 new contacts.

What's lying around?

Take a note of everything you have already amassed throughout your life that might help towards your goal of running a successful business: all the little things you thought you'd buy and put aside for a rainy day, all the presents taking up room under the stairs. Whatever your idea for a business, you may have 90% of what you need right there in your own home, lurking under the stairs, in the shed, in the attic or, most importantly, in your head.

Trashion House

Trashion is the art of taking rubbish and turning it into wearable clothing, furniture and objects of desire. The rubbish you use may be curtains, old CDs, jewellery, seashells—there's no end to the trash you can use to make new items. Build a website for free that showcases the photographs of your best pieces and sell them on. Create a buzz about your Trashion brand. Look at rubbish in a new light and see its potential as a money maker.

Below are some typical lists of what you might have right now that can serve a dual role when re-employed in your new business.

Stuff in your house

→ Paper
→ Laptop computer
→ Broadband
→ Mobile phone
→ Pens
→ Chairs
→ Business suit
→ Telephone landline

Stuff in your life

→ Family
→ Friends

→ Readymade network in a different industry
→ Competitive information
→ Credibility within your current industry
→ Credibility within your peer group
→ Car
→ Bike

Stuff in your head

→ Ideas
→ Confidence
→ Focus
→ Emotion
→ Personality
→ Deep IT skills
→ Presentation skills
→ Sales skills
→ Interpersonal (soft) skills
→ Freedom
→ Creativity
→ Shopping list

When you know what you have already in your campaign armoury, then you can start thinking about what you haven't got. It's a very good start to note this down as well, as this will be the source of information for the next few chapters. How do you get hold of what you need without paying any money for it?

Here's what I didn't have on my list when I started my first company. It makes you wonder how I started in the first place!

→ Investment
→ Income
→ Financial skills
→ Prototype/product
→ Customers
→ Production
→ Suppliers
→ Industry knowledge
→ Credibility

Make two lists:

1. Everything you currently have on hand to start and run your business.
2. Everything you think you need to run and grow your business.

One of the fundamental benefits of being an entrepreneur can be summed up in the following wise words from Jim Rohn, an American entrepreneur and speaker on personal development:

The greatest reward in becoming a millionaire is not the amount of money that you earn. It is the kind of person that you have to become to become a millionaire in the first place.

When you start a business and understand the true nature of entrepreneurship, you want to use the skills you have gained, mostly the hard way, over and over again. In relation to the freesourcing ethic, you want to save money and maximize profits throughout your entrepreneurial career. That's why you will always need to appraise a situation and see where to save money and maximize profits. So once you have learnt the benefits of drawing up the above lists, you'll do it on a regular basis.

Obviously, I have no idea what you have lying around. However, the average value of a person's worldly goods at any one time (excluding property, savings and investments) is believed to be a mere 22% of their annual income. So, say, **£25,000** × 22% = **£5,500**.

Creativity

Are you creative? Of course you are! It's just that a lot of people have simply forgotten how.

When you were a child, you would happily concentrate for hours on end, creating endless scenarios played out with the tools you had to hand: building blocks, dolls, cars, trains, dressing-up clothes and action heroes. The creativity you had as a child was a powerful tool that you could call on to bring you happiness and that acted as comfort and support.

You still have this capacity for creative thought, but it may be buried deep down and the "toys" are different. You need to release your creativity and enjoy the benefits it brings you in business.

One trick is to exercise your brain and perhaps think a little more like a child. Do a simple crossword, paint a picture, sing a song, read some poetry, kick a ball about. Enjoy the freedom of letting go of your worries.

You may already have an idea for a business or just an inkling of one. Take this spark, get some quiet time and see if you can let your mind wander into unexpected places. When you get good at this, the brain begins to reorganize your thoughts for you. Typically, the dream state is the mind's way of allocating space and links to the thoughts and experiences you have been having throughout the day. Dreams are often a strange collection of follow-on events because your brain is making subconscious connections. Practice creativity and you can enable this process in your waking brain, making subconscious connections to solve complex problems without much effort. All it takes is a little practice.

Thomas Edison used to exercise his creativity by doing his thinking in a comfortable chair with a few ball bearings in his hand, draped over the armrest. If he fell asleep, the ball bearings would drop into a metal receptacle and the clattering would wake him up. He believed that his most potent ideas came from the time between waking and sleeping, when his mind was able to set his thoughts free. How many times have you fretted over a problem and then nodded off to sleep, only to find in the morning that the solution was there all along? That's your brain doing its work. Sometimes it's better not to force a solution out but to coax it out with a little quiet time.

Your brain is a remarkable asset. Learn how to use it effectively and it could be the best freesource tool you ever find.

Apalachee Bay, Paris

Two enterprising business associates started a business in Paris with no money. They had the idea when looking for a flat to rent in the city. There is a very well-known location called the American Church, which had a noticeboard that was updated daily with new and available flats for rent at reasonable prices.

The two enterprising entrepreneurs took it upon themselves to create a company that rented flats in Paris, called Apalachee Bay. As a starting point, they took note of all the properties for rent and made their own free advert, which they posted back on the noticeboard. They then took down the original postings. When travellers came along looking for flats to rent, the lads' number was prominently displayed on the otherwise empty noticeboard. The travellers had nowhere else to turn but Apalachee Bay, which very kindly organized rentals for them and also handled the business end for people wanting to rent out their flats.

First a warning: your business ethics are up to you, but it is vital for the longevity of your business to ensure that you conduct your business in a fair and credible manner. But there are also a couple of good ideas to be taken from this approach. The boys knew that they had a flow of continually updated new business, as the American Church was already the place to go for flat lettings. And they saw the opportunity and went for it, even though they had no experience in this area. The two friends are now enjoying the fruits of their labour after the sale of their business in 2000.

Ways around a problem always exist, you just need to be creative. Go back to basics and ask *why* things have to be done a certain way. Don't be bullied by the mainstream, challenge authority with creative reasoning. Be a grown-up child.

When faced with a supplier telling you they have never carried out a piece of work in a certain way, ask: "Why not?" Use your ignorance or lack of experience in a situation to your advantage: "Why does it have to be done that way?" It's not fair for the supplier to impose restrictions in their terms and conditions, so tell them that. Unlike kids, you can justify your questions with experienced reasoning.

Your creativity is one of your most powerful free assets. It's how the human race grows and adapts to situations seemingly beyond its control. If you can learn to harness this extremely powerful freesource, you can creatively overcome any issue and move on with your business.

If you get stuck and need some on-the-fly inspiration, I can wholeheartedly recommend the TED website (www.ted. com). TED stands for Technology, Education, Design. A TED Conference is held annually and is an invitation-only event where the world's leading thinkers and doers gather to find inspiration. The only two requirements for TED talks are that the topic must be novel and that the speech lasts no longer than 18 minutes. The TED website has only recently begun sharing these talks with the rest of the world in video podcasts. You can now participate in a melting pot of unbelievable creativity. If it's quick inspiration you're after, then look no further to stimulate your creative thinking.

 Creativity learning course, mind stimulation and brainaware seminar: **£250**.

Emotion

Smile, you have something that no one can take away from you: your emotion. You have real feeling and hunger for the success of your project. The emotional value that you can put into the project is a powerful tool when focused correctly. You can build on it to drive the idea forward, grow the business and achieve your goals. It's all very "Eye of the Tiger" and, best of all, you don't have to pay for it. You just have to believe in yourself and let your emotion work the way that best suits your personality.

Investors love entrepreneurs. In many cases they love the entrepreneur more than the idea they are trying to get off the ground. It's the person who can make things happen, not the idea alone. So it's you who will be the success of your project. You are the most powerful person in your organization. Isn't that why you started it in the first place?

Entrepreneurs who start their business for more than just money are far more likely to succeed, purely because they are driven by an emotional goal rather than a financial one. Do footballers start out by saying "I'm going to become a millionaire football player" or do they play, live and breathe football because they love the feelings and emotions they associate with the game they have real talent for? Being successful at something you love has to be more of a reward than simply the money alone. So work out *why* you want to start your business.

One of the simplest free resources you can have is a positive mental attitude. Look online for self-motivation blogs and detailed business case studies that involve emotion. And think about this quote from the author Ashleigh Brilliant, who can see the sunny side of every situation:

> *Living on earth may be expensive but at least it includes an annual free trip around the sun.*

It's important to remember that emotion in business dealings breeds confidence, but it can also cloud your judgement about a situation. Use the emotion to succeed to drive your understanding of every situation you find yourself in, and question each decision you take to ensure you are being objective rather than subjective in your overall approach.

Talent, emotion, drive, determination and focus are the keys here—how much do you have to pay to benefit from these qualities? Nothing, because it's all already inside you, bursting to get out.

Freeq

20 sessions with a business coach, psychologist or life coach at £50 an hour: **£1000**.

The art of barter

We talked about bartering your time earlier, but there are other possibilities. Before money was available, bartering was the preferred system for exchanging goods and services. In fact, in some countries bartering is still the main mechanism, such as those where money is no longer a viable exchange medium or societies where money has no meaning. And the great news for the freesourcer is that in the modern world, as people try to cut costs and increase margins, bartering as a trading mechanism is on the rise.

In bartering, goods or services are directly exchanged for other goods or services, without the use of money. As a very simple example, I have two hours to spare and you can pay me to help you collect eggs with a dozen of those eggs. I can then either sell the eggs on to someone in exchange for cash, make them into an omelette with other raw materials and sell the product and my cooking service on to some clients at a greater profit, or just boil some eggs and feed my family. After all, eggs is eggs, as they say.

When researching this book I looked for a barter transaction request. Within three minutes on a simple web search for "free computer," I found this on craigslist (http://craigslist.co.uk):

Who wants a free computer? XXXX is putting together our "Build 6" program. You build five computers and take the sixth one home for free! NO EXPERIENCE NECESSARY. By the time you get to your sixth box you'll be an expert.

The company gets five computers built for the price of the raw materials of a single computer. Everyone wins, which is one of the main tenets of freesourcing.

Bartering is more than simply doing someone a favour, but favours are something you should work into your bartering schedule to elicit the law of threefold return. This states that anything you do for or to someone else will be revisited on you at a later time with three times the original input. If you hit your little brother because he stole your sweets, he will retaliate and hit you three times harder, and so on until the inevitable tears happen.

In business it works the same way, and the opportunity of a beneficial threefold return is something you can learn how to leverage. Say you offer to help someone in their business for a day and ask nothing for it but the experience and skills you learn from working in the environment. The proprietor will not forget this and will inevitably, when the time is right, repay this favour with more than you might expect. People remember things that impress them and associate this with a value when the time comes to repay the favour. Never underestimate the power of volunteering.

Organizations have been set up to increase the use of global bartering, such as Bartercard. The idea is a great one, and although there is a cost involved, this is guaranteed to be repaid in terms of new business for your company within the first year of joining. If Bartercard is unable to get you more business than the amount you paid at sign-up, the company returns your initial sign-up fee. This essentially makes the service free. I particularly like the way in which

Bartercard promotes your business to other members, like a specialized networking club. When you sign up for the service you are offered an interest-free line of credit initially up to T£3000 (T£ being trade pounds, the online currency of the Bartercard system). Go to www.bartercard.com for more details.

The global airline companies and large hotel chains have been bartering for years. The airlines offer empty seats on their aircraft to hotels so that they can tie in deals for both travel and accommodation. In return, airline staff are allowed to stay for free anywhere in the world on stopovers, which is a fantastic benefit for the carriers. Everyone benefits from the spare capacity.

Kyle Macdonald began bartering on 12 July 2005. His goal was to see if he could start with a red paperclip and continue bartering until he managed to trade up to a house. On 12 July 2006, 14 trades later, he did indeed manage to bag himself a house, 503 Main St, Kipling, Saskatchewan. Here's how he did it:

1. Red paperclip
2. Fish pen
3. Door knob
4. Colman stove
5. Red generator
6. Instant party
7. Famous skidoo
8. Trip to Yahk
9. Cube van

10. Recording contract
11. Year in Phoenix
12. Afternoon with Alice Cooper
13. KISS snowglobe
14. Movie role
15. House

Could Kyle Macdonald be the King of Trades?

Your spare capacity might be your time or your excess production. Use trade exchanges to minimize losses to your business and gain new customers.

Hotel room swapped for an airline ticket: **£150**.

Experience

Not everyone reading this book will have worked before, but the vast majority will have carried out some work for payment in the past. Everything you experience, both good and bad, may be beneficial to your learning and therefore to the knowledge you need when starting up a business. Learn from every situation, seek out the reasons things worked and other things failed and put that knowledge to use.

If your current work experience is the catalyst for your business idea, use your time to see how your employers do things, test the boundaries of their operation and try things out while you can. Test your ideas and theories on someone else's time rather than your own, before you leave employment and start out on your own.

Experiences build confidence: if you have faced something before then it may not seem so daunting a second time. This can work in all kinds of situations, from negotiating a large deal to standing in front of an audience about to deliver a presentation.

If you cannot experience a situation before it happens, a great tool for preparing yourself is to visualize what is likely to happen and work out an outcome based on what you do know. Perhaps you are about to enter into a meeting to close the sale of a licence for your software and consulting services. Play out the scenario in your head. Have you asked if this is the meeting for the agreement to go ahead and contracts to be signed? What if they say no? How will you react: will you drop your shoulders and look disappointed, or will you ask why not and see if there's an obstacle you can remove? What could the obstacle be? Worse still, what if they say yes? How are you going to react then? What is an expected reaction to good news? Jumping up and down on the table and screaming "thank-you, thank-you, thank-you, I love you" is not a strategy I advise.

The message is clear. Calmly think through the likely scenario and what the possible outcomes might be. Prepare for those outcomes and visualize a successful conclusion. This free technique is used by business people and athletes alike to prepare them for the unexpected and, more importantly, for the expected results they will achieve.

When you decide to start a business in an industry in which you have had experience, create a product to use to advertise yourself. If you are a website designer, create a website for yourself and showcase your talents. If you are an accountant, manage your finances cleverly and create a case study to show to your prospects. You are your business, so use yourself as the showcase for what you can achieve for your clients.

Freestart

Business consultant

Sell consultancy services based on your expertise in your existing industry. Show people in the same and similar industries how to do things more efficiently and for less cost. Make sure you have a track record of success and convert your CV/resumé into a biography worthy to be employed on a day rate basis to help organizations improve their business practice.

Keep your expertise up to date and find new ways for your industry to succeed by visiting exhibitions and conferences tailored to your requirements. Network well at these events and always call those people who showed even the tiniest inkling of interest. You will need to ensure that you're networking at the right levels of an organization, so aim high and punch above your weight by competing against larger organizations that may already be the contractor of choice.

Write articles for trade magazines to increase your credibility and convert these articles into white papers on specific topics—White paper titles might include "Increase your sales performance using XXX", for example—that you can send out to prospects as a sales tool. Get in touch with companies whose tools you plan to use to implement your consulting solution. Get them to train you in the latest techniques and in return you have a portfolio of options for your new customers and a possible revenue stream selling add-ons to the tools you provide.

As businesses you have consulted for change and take on new staff, approach the customer again to see if the plan you implemented is still working, if their people need extra training and what other services you can offer.

Freeq All-singing, all-dancing, three-page website created by a professional designer: **£1000**.

Prices and negotiation

When you walk into a shop, whatever kind of shop, you instantly know if something is good value or not. You've probably bought items every day of your adult life and you instinctively know when an item is priced too high or very keenly. Do you negotiate in the supermarket? No, because supermarkets represent good value for money. Do you negotiate in an electrical retailer? No, but you should do! Did you know that nearly every high street branded retail manager has an automatic 10% discretionary discount available to any customer who asks? Give it a try, especially for high-priced items such as televisions, vacuum cleaners and watches. This is your money we're talking about. You need to get into the habit of negotiating early on in your start-up.

Business works on a single principle: the price of a product fluctuates in response to how much you need it. I've chosen my words carefully here, because need is different to want. We all want a second home in the sun, but do we actually need it? When someone needs a new heart I'm pretty sure they would mortgage the house to pay for the transplant. What you have to make sure you learn is that you must swap your desires or wants for needs. Only buy things when you *need* them.

Every time you buy something, whether a product or a service, try this experiment in your head or, when appropriate, directly with the seller. Ask what the free option is. In most cases the free option is not having the product or service at all, but this simple question serves as an excellent reminder to you that there should always be a free or discounted option available. It doesn't hurt to try, it's just a question of confidence. I've often been offered demonstration models at 30% discount or more, just because I asked if there were any demonstration models for sale.

Everything is negotiable: it's up to you to get the best possible deals in everything you do. This means in your business and also for your personal purchases. Save money by asking for a discount. People can only say no.

 25% discount on printed marketing flyers at **£100** for 5000: **£25** saving (or 1250 free flyers).

The entrepreneurial advantage

The entrepreneurial advantage represents the advantage you have right now over larger businesses that you may aspire to compete against. Right now, even though you've only just made the decision to go ahead with your business idea, you already have some great advantages over your competition in the marketplace. How much confidence does this give you to keep going and build on the idea further?

Your entrepreneurial advantage includes the following features:

→ You are unique: the collection of experiences you have had up to now are unique to you. For example, you may have the eyes to see opportunities and inventions that others might miss.
→ You have the passion to make this idea happen. Only two thirds of employees actually enjoy their job. You have the advantage of passion for your business, driving you forward every day.

→ You are flexible. It may take some large companies, with all their huge resources, months and many signatures from the hierarchy of managers and directors to get a new idea into production.

→ You have a short decision-making process. You are responsible for the business and are not looking to advance or safeguard your career—the buck stops here and you can press the button now.

→ You have low overheads, particularly because you are using freesourcing to drive your business. This means two things: you can be much more competitive on price while maintaining quality; and you can enjoy a better margin on sales.

→ You can engage one to one with suppliers and customers. You are your business and you can use this to your advantage in negotiations and speed of supply. As the business owner, you can create excellent, personal customer service rather than being a representative of a large commercial organization.

→ You are your brand. Use your reputation as a competitive advantage.

Revel in your confidence and realize that you do have massive advantages over larger businesses. In many respects large businesses are nervous of start-ups, as these may turn out to be their future competitors in the marketplace. Try to work under the radar, just out of sight of prying competitive eyes, until you are ready to launch, so that possible competitive organizations will not have time to react should you have that blockbuster idea that will rock the foundations of their happy world.

 Setting up a business and running it for 20 years: **£2.5 m+**

This chapter has been about using what you have. For many start-ups this is solely a matter of time and effort. For other businesses it's about product design and intellectual property. Whatever business you decide to start, make sure that you are not spending money unnecessarily on things you just don't need to get the business going. Yes, it is nice to have flashy business cards, an all-encompassing website and a nice office to do your work in, but ask yourself if these are the ideals you aspire to or things you actually require right now.

Total Freeq Value

Circa **£9,000**

(with the £2.5 m taken out!)

2

Setting Up the Foundations of Your Business

The more you act like a business, the more people will believe that you are a business. Very simply, as with anything in life, the more you say and do, the more real it becomes. It's very easy to say "I am an entrepreneur," but what you have to be is a *successful* entrepreneur, thinking like a true business mogul and making sure that you build your business in the right way from the ground up.

Strong foundations build a strong company. This chapter is all about getting the fundamentals right and, most importantly, setting off on the right foot with your understanding of freesourcing.

Ask yourself: Why am I starting the business? What kind of business do I want to start? What do I want to achieve and can I achieve it? If you don't know where you want to get to, then how can you make a plan to get there? Have a broad but flexible plan. You are in charge, so make sure you listen to the boss.

Elevator pitch

What is your business about? You need to be able to convey exactly what your business service or product is in around 10 to 30 seconds. That's not an easy exercise, but it is, to my mind, probably the most important piece of the jigsaw. When you meet people at networking events and they ask what you do, a quick snappy answer will produce the best results. Any mumbling and bumbling lets you down. If you are unable to put into words exactly what you do, then how do you expect to convey the right meaning to someone who may have never come across a similar business or service? Even if you're talking to someone who doesn't have a need for what you do, they may know someone else who does. Make your ideas worth spreading by making them easy to understand.

It can be fun coming up with an elevator pitch, but once you've completed it, you will have the basis for communicating your idea in simple and memorable terms. Get it down on paper. You need to live and breathe your product or service.

A really memorable way to introduce two people who you know, but who have never met each other before, is to create a personal elevator pitch for each one. For example:

"Nik, I would like to introduce you to Jason. Jason lives in Surrey and finds new homes for premiership footballers when they transfer to a new club and he enjoys mountain biking and skiing."

"Jason, Nik is an international event organizer for blue-chip companies specializing in the latest telecommunications technology. She lives in Ilkley with her husband Jim and their six children."

Both contacts are introduced and then it's up to them to get on with explaining their businesses and how they might be able to help each other using the common ground you have laid down.

Make it easy for people to meet each other. If it goes well then you will always be remembered as the one who introduced them in the first place. If you can do this with everyone you meet, you'll be a networking giant. Keep notes on the back of people's business cards to remind you.

You can practice developing an elevator pitch by taking existing products and trying to formulate a business introduction that the inventor might have used when pitching the idea to investors and customers, before the product became mainstream. I've used this as a game in many seminars and courses on public speaking and entrepreneurship.

Imagine pitching to people who have never seen or heard of these types of products before:

- A hula hoop
- The first mobile phone
- A hammer
- Bottled water

Here are my elevator pitches for these products:

Hula hoop

A hula hoop is a plastic ring used both as an exercise regime for adults and as a child's plaything. The hoop works by the hooper (the person using the hula hoop) rotating their hips with the hula hoop located around their waist. The game is to see how long they are able to keep it spinning without letting the hoop fall to the ground. This helps users tone their bodies and provides endless hours of fun at a low cost. The name came from the traditional Hawaiian islands' dance, the hula.

Mobile phone

The mobile phone is a portable wireless communications device that customers use to make one-to-one calls to both traditional telephones and other mobile phone users using wireless networks powered by telephony service providers.

Hammer

A hammer is a low-cost product made of traditional materials (with a metal head and a wooden shaft), which a user employs, together with nails, in order to create a strong bond between wooden structures. The hammer is used to strike a nail into a section of wood anywhere along its length.

Bottled water

Bottled water is a liquid product made from hydrogen and oxygen, manufactured by natural processes and bottled for resale in a portable plastic container. Customers like bottled water because it rehydrates and refreshes naturally on the go. The product is naturally occurring, cheap to produce and has a seemingly endless supply of raw material. Water is a vital component for the survival of all life.

There are many elevator pitch competitions: for example, have a look at www.startupnation.com and navigate to its annual elevator pitch competition. Why not video yourself and upload the pitch to YouTube, then send an email to investors? Or register for cmypitch.com (http://cmypitch.com), which will host your pitch and provide the opportunity for angel investors to view it. The site offers other services as well, all for free:

→ A supplier sourcing service called Quick Quotes, which saves on making calls to find relevant suppliers who would like your business.
→ A video-based advice centre.
→ Video interviews with top entrepreneurs.
→ Price comparisons on banking, utilities and insurance.

When you use your elevator pitch in the real world, sparks of interest can lead people to ask for further details. Move the business conversation forward to explore the opportunities for both parties. You may have made an easy sale without realizing it.

 1 day of a professional copywriter's time learning about your business and creating an elevator pitch for you: **£100**.

The legal entity

A first time freesourcer will most likely opt to create a business entity around the sole trader option until such time as the business grows and they are willing to spend £20 on setting up a limited company, with all the benefits this brings.

Browse the Companies House website (www.companie shouse.gov.uk) to get a feel for what kind of company you would like to start and what type you can start for free.

There's a wealth of help on this subject, so ensure you do your research and start the entity that's right for you. Ask to have a meeting with a Business Link adviser (www.businesslink.gov.uk), who can suggest the best option for your business future.

You should probably take some advice on the subject from a professional. It's rather handy that nearly all professionals will give you an hour of their time for free.

Freeq   Registering a limited company: **£20.**

Using professional help

Professionals have earned the right to advise you on a number of speciality topics based on years of experience and study. However, every person who is paid for their time can be called a professional, so don't do yourself down: you are a professional in your own right.

Professionals will more often than not offer you a limited amount of free advice on a particular topic if requested. This works as a sales meeting and during the meeting they hope to convey to you that they are more than capable of looking after your ongoing issues.

Most professionals charge by the hour (some by the sixth of an hour; that is, every 10 minutes), so the usual free opportunity here is for an hour only. If you want to take this route, you must prepare thoroughly to ensure that you maximize the time spent on discovering new information about the area you want to explore.

A sneaky freesourcer might hop from professional to professional, honing the issue each time and getting more and more information, so that they eventually solve the problem outright without paying a penny. However, this is a little underhand and everyone needs to make a living, so the freesourcing ethic doesn't condone it. Ensure you have trawled the Internet and searched all the relevant books before you ask someone to spend a free hour of their time helping you out and solve a particular problem. This is simply professional courtesy.

 1 hour of a specialist intellectual property lawyer's time: **£150**.

Business plan

The creation of a business plan is vital to the success of your start-up. As a project it forces you to ask yourself difficult questions and find rational and impartial answers. The document sets the tone of the business and acts as an ongoing and ever-changing guide.

You can prepare for this in several ways. Read the many blogs and websites dedicated to showing you how to build the perfect business plan. Download a business plan template from your local Business Link (www.businesslink.gov.uk). Watch business programmes like *Dragons' Den* and see what questions they ask the entrepreneurs.

These are the questions you should be asking yourself:

→ Who is the management team and why are they the right people to start the business?
→ What funds does the business have (in our case £0)?
→ What are the assets of the business, the products, services and entities in the business that we have amassed already?
→ What is the estimated market size for this business?
→ How are we going to market our product or service via the business?
→ Do we already have customers, if so how many and what is the estimated revenue?
→ What is our elevator pitch?
→ What is the first year's detailed cash-flow forecast?
→ What is the detailed first-year profit and loss account?
→ What is the three-year profit and loss account?
→ What is our exit strategy to reap the rewards of the business?
→ What intellectual property rights have we registered?

If you can answer all of these in a detailed and methodical manner in a document of no more than 15 pages, then you have the makings of a fine business plan. All it takes is time and detail to get your business plan in place; two things that you have for free.

In the UK there are over 3000 colleges of higher education, universities and advanced learning institutions. Of these, 93% offer a business course for a varying target audience. If you would like to get your business plan looked over, submit it to the tutors and lecturers of the business faculty and ask them to use it as a case study with their classes and tutor groups. They will love picking it apart in minute detail and getting their class to do the same. Can you imagine having 20 pairs of impartial eyes looking over your work? The idea is nerve-racking, to say the least. But these fresh eyes will give you insight into your own understanding of the business plan.

What do you want to do with your business plan? Your answer is probably one of two things:

→ You might be setting up the business by yourself, so you will use the business plan as a moving and ever-changing map to steer you towards your goal. If this is the case, then letting the business faculty look over your pride and joy will be like having 20 consultants advising you on strategies for your business for free!

→ Your plan might act as a window on the investment opportunity you offer to business angels or funding agencies. If this is the case, you *must* ensure that the plan is as tightly held together as possible, so another set of eyes cast over the work is invaluable for pointing out the questions that investors might ask along the way. If you can prepare answers to these questions, you have taken the risk out of every angle that may encourage a potential investor to say no.

A business plan is a strategy for the future, an ever-changing beast of a document that acts as your ongoing guide to business success. It should be vital to your everyday operations and tactics. Don't lose sight of the fact that this document represents the business before the business itself takes off, so take the utmost care in preparing it and making it work for you.

Asking an accountant to spend a week of their time helping you prepare a business plan: **£2500** (or 5% of your shiny new company!).

A place to work

In order for you to conduct your day-to-day business, you require a secure and peaceful office to work from, somewhere you can go and feel you are "at work," a place to spend your day working on the things that are most important to the future of your business. Don't you?

It would be lovely if we all had a readymade office, a private place to go and contemplate the difficulties of the day. But in fact all you need is a table and a chair; sometimes you don't even need that.

Your business address is your home address—get used to it. Global Super Mega Corp Ltd, 237 Acacia Avenue, Norwich. This is where you do your business. You don't need an office right now, you already have an address, so tailor it to suit your needs.

Be creative with the address you use for your business. My first business address was Santeau Ltd, Unit 39 WCT, when in fact my home address at the time was 39 Westcliffe Terrace. The Post Office always delivered. Then I upgraded and got myself a PO Box, even though I think that some-times feels a little impersonal.

Sarah Feather Design

After leaving college with a degree in textile design, Sarah Feather didn't have a single job interview. Instead, she had her collection photographed, created some flyers and took her products, ranging from wall hangings to birthday cards, round the industry. She had very cleverly hit on a unique method for preserving fruit and incorporating it into her textile designs. There was nothing like it on the market and she had orders flooding in even before she started finding out where to manufacture the products that were being requested. She took advance orders and from her own home created the Sarah Feather brand and offered work to out-sourced seamstresses, to whom she taught the process. The outworkers knew they would only be paid when she was paid. Now her clients include up-market department stores such as Harrods and Neiman Marcus.

If you have a spare room, use that; if not then use your kitchen table; if you haven't got a kitchen table, then get one for free. Sahar Hashemi founded Coffee Republic with her brother Bobby from her kitchen table and even named her book after it. I am currently writing this book on a veranda outside a ski chalet in Chamonix in the French Alps (actually that's a fib, I'm at my kitchen table too, but we all need a dream). It's what you do at your business address that counts, not the address itself.

If you don't want to work at home, there are other places to get the peace and quiet you need. Some ideas for a free-sourced workplace:

→ A friend's workplace might have a spare desk, just go and ask if you can use it for a while.
→ The local library is not only a fount of knowledge but also a quiet place to sit and get on with work, especially research.
→ If you have a current job, stay late and use the space there, but be discreet. Ask permission if you can; maybe tell people you're working on a friend's event and need to get the organization done.
→ Hotel lobbies and seating areas are great places to make calls, meet people and do your daily business tasks. Such areas are free apart from tea, coffee, food and meeting rooms, and they often have free wifi connections.

Entrepreneurship is all about taking advantage of ever-changing market conditions, so it's easy to see how the pop-up phenomenon emerged. When the country is in a recession, staying in is always the new going out. But for £25 a head and BYOB (bring your own booze), you can pop round to a nearby house where they've created an ad hoc restaurant in their front room. Word of mouth has spread the message and there will be friends, neighbours and even people from far and wide who've come to sample the delights of the hosts' offerings.

The organizers have to order in food, but the premises are essentially free because it's their house. Even variable service is forgivable because you're eating at someone else's house! The host expects to clear about £500–700 in one evening's work—great for a budding chef who can't yet afford their own premises.

Freestart

Pop Up Restaurant

You enjoy cooking for family and friends and have been complimented on your dinner parties, so why not start getting paid for them by opening your own restaurant? Post a note on craigslist (http://craigslist.co.uk) or perhaps a foodie forum saying you have 12 tickets to sell for an underground *paladares*-style pop-up restaurant. This is a restaurant that you operate from your own home, named after what they are called in Cuba, where the movement began.

You will have to set up a website detailing what the menu will consist of and when the event will take place, and perhaps give the evening a theme. You can sell the tickets in advance online through a PayPal account, to pay for the food that you serve on the night. People bring their own drinks, you charge them just for the meal and service. Don't worry that your organization might be a little scrappy at first, as this adds to the mystique and adventure for the customers. If you want to run more than one meal, keep the word of mouth going by sending your guests home with a present as part of a themed evening.

However, the adventure is not just for the customers: remember that you will be allowing strangers into your home and you may want to delay releasing the location details until you have sold all the tickets. The legal position of these restaurants is also still somewhat unclear, so you need to take advice on such issues as health and safety and insurance if you want to do this on a regular basis.

Another recent development is pop-up shops, retail outlets that are rented for a short amount of time and make money out of a very fast stock turn. Many pop-up shops are branded and use the Internet to announce the next town they intend to visit. They have been widely used by the fashion industry to create a local buzz for high-end couture clothing and accessories.

 Rented small restaurant with kitchen facilities: **£2500** per calendar month.

Money

All start-ups think they need money. I hope, when you have read all of this book, that you will see that you don't actually need any money to start a business. Nevertheless, as a business grows there is bound to be a need for cash to support that growth and to invest in new products and services, as well as in the business processes to streamline your organization and make it more competitive.

However, there are some standard ways to use the financial system to your advantage. Making money may not be the reason you started out on your own, but your dealings with money will be a consequence of doing business.

Let's clear one thing up right now. When I'm talking about free money, I mean money that you don't have to earn or pay back, at least not straight away.

Credit card finance

One of the traditional methods of getting so-called free money is to sign up to an interest-free credit card. The only drawback with this is that you will certainly have to pay the money back at some stage, hopefully when the business is rocking and the money is rolling in.

Mum of three and past graduate of a very influential London dance school, Vik wanted to go back to work. It didn't take too long for her to realize that she didn't fancy being stuck in an office environment but felt the urge to dance again. In order to fit her working time around the kids, she thought it would be a great idea, like many mompreneurs, to start up on her own and on her own terms.

With her passion for dance and love of children, she created the Dance Project, an after-school dance activity aimed at young kids wanting to learn the rudiments of street dance. As an active member of the local school, she used her mums' word-of-mouth network to research the idea and managed to get a couple of friends to sign their children up for the inaugural lesson. She then approached the school and asked if she could offer the project through its facilities.

In order to run the first event, Vik had to ensure she had the right insurance, clothes, music and a few other bits and pieces that she needed to get going. However, with no money this did not seem a likely event. But in true free-sourcing style, she took on a new credit card offering 0% APR for six months, free money as long as it's paid off in time! The event went ahead as planned and was a great success. Vik paid off the credit card straight away and cut it up so she wouldn't use it again. The Dance Project now runs four times a week and has created over 250 new introductions to street dance.

Stoozing

Stoozing is a method of making money from credit cards with a time-limited 0% finance deal. Loads of readily accessible credit cards lend new customers money at 0% for between 6 and 16 months, after which time interest is applied to any outstanding balance. To stooze, you transfer the balance from the credit card and stash it in a high-interest savings account, one with as high a rate of interest as possible. Now you're earning interest on the money the credit card company has lent you for free.

Make sure you keep an eye on when the interest-free period expires and pay back the balance to ensure you do not have to pay anything for it. The savings account will have earned interest over the period and this, after tax, is pure profit, literally making money from nothing. If you do this for a couple of years with different cards before starting your business, you will have some extra cash to help you move forward on the first rungs of the ladder. Remember, this is freesourcing, so don't spend the cash, save it.

Savings

If you do have savings, use them for your business. This is money you've put away to secure your financial future or to dip into on a rainy day. Why not use it (very wisely indeed) to assure your financial security by starting a business with this easily accessible pot of cash, in the knowledge that you will be paid back many times over when your business starts to make money.

Inheritance

If your parents have money and you have a good relationship with them, then why not ask for your inheritance up front when you need it most? They will be able to see what you can do with the business and be proud that they're still around to see it. There is a benefit for Ma and Pa stepping in and helping out, as in the UK under current laws, any gift given more than seven years before a person's death is not subject to inheritance tax, which can represent a massive long-term saving. Don't forget that you do have to declare it correctly to HM Revenue and Customs.

Bootstrapping

Bootstrapping is one step beyond freesourcing. You minimize your start-up costs by working in another environment or starting another business to make money that you can reinvest in the main business that you are really eager to create. Bootstrapping might be as straightforward as working for an employer in a traditional employee role and putting money away until such time as you feel you can start your main venture.

Shorttask (www.shorttask.com) has loads of micro-jobs that can earn you money in your spare time. You decide when you want to work on the tasks you choose and get a reward for doing them. These are not the most stimulating roles available and they don't pay megabucks, but they do offer flexibility and can generate an income to set aside for starting your own business one day.

Buying and selling

Here is as good a place as any to introduce Martin Lewis, whose name may already be familiar to you. Martin runs the aptly named MoneySavingExpert.com website and forums (http://forums.moneysavingexpert.com). Martin offers heaps of advice on how to save money and organize your personal finances, which can be mapped directly onto your business life as well. As Martin puts it on his website:

A company's job is to make money. A consumer's job is maximize their cash. Companies spend billions on advertising, marketing and teaching their staff to sell; yet we don't get buyers' training.

I agree wholeheartedly with Martin on this one. Consumers don't get buyers' training, but many companies do. If you are going to source excellent-value products for your own business use, then you have to become an expert buyer.

Visit Martin's site and have a good nose around. There's a wealth of useful information and something there for everyone.

Earlier in the book I asked you to find all the stuff lying around that might be useful to your business. You very cleverly took this advice and have separated all your possessions into mental piles:

- Stuff I can use for my business.
- Stuff I need for my life.
- Other stuff that is not really of any use whatsoever so I'll bin it.

Wait! Don't throw out all those weight-loss DVDs and oven gloves in the shape of a hippo. Instead, use them to add to your cash-stash war chest. You could always sell them at a car boot sale or on eBay, which I talk about later in the book, but there are also many shops nationwide that can convert unwanted presents, old CDs and all the bits and pieces you have lying around into hard cash.

One such outlet with about 120 stores around the UK is the aptly named Cash Converters, to be found at the equally aptly named website www.cashconverters.co.uk. Its aim is to be a second-hand goods store that works like a professional retail outlet. Not only can you sell your stuff at Cash Converters, you can also get your hands on some pre-owned bargains for your new business. See if you can swap your old, useless stuff for some office equipment or other bits and pieces that you need.

 **Freeq** Immeasurable cash is cash, try to keep hold of it!

Travel

Getting to meetings on time is one professional skill that is imperative to your business and personal credibility and shows how serious you are approaching your business. An essential freesourcing rule is always to be on time. Wasting other people's time is rude and unprofessional and there's never a good enough excuse for being late.

Your method of free transport will depend on the distance you need to travel:

- 0–2 miles: walk.
- 1–5 miles: cycle.
- 5–250 miles: carshare (check out www.liftshare.com/uk or www.carshare.com).

➜ 250–3000 miles: very cheap flights secured eight months in advance when you only pay the taxes. (This kind of flight is often impossible to get at very short notice, although you never know, so check out lastminute.com and other late booking services).

Carshare schemes work on the basis that someone in your area is travelling to a destination that you also want to get to. You contact them and agree that they will pick you up and take you to that location (but remember, they may not necessarily be coming back your way). Fuel costs are shared equally and that's that. Payment for fuel does not necessarily have to be hard cash: you could agree to do a chore for the person in advance or take them something that is of equal monetary value.

Carsharing is different to—and safer than—hitchhiking, which is still alive and well although in decline in the UK. Remember that if you do decide to use a carshare scheme, always let a friend or relative know where you are going, with whom and when you expect to be back.

The best way to avoid travelling costs entirely is to ask people to come to you, either to your home, your shared office or neutral ground such as a hotel. People love a good excuse to get out of the office once in a while, so make your offer compelling enough to draw them out.

You can also avoid travel costs with online meetings and seminars, which enable us all to WFH (work from home). Unbelievably, there are even tools to make your WFH videos and conference calls sound as if they are being made from a work environment, to give your work-from-home crew a more authentic feel. For a good example, go to www. thrivingoffice.com. Instead of buying a CD like this, just go and record a work environment that suits your needs. The person on the other end of the phone will believe that your organization has hundreds of people tirelessly working towards the common goal of corporate success.

Freeq 400-mile car journey: **£40** (and that's just the petrol).

Sourcing equipment

It's time to mention the mighty Freecycle (www.freecycle. org). This is a website where people just like you and me give away our unwanted items for free, at no cost, gratis. Instead of taking items down to the tip or dumping them next to the railway sidings, people would rather know that their stuff is being put to good use.

The success of the website is down to its simplicity. You must first become a member of a local group and subscribe to the relevant email list. You will receive about 50 emails every day with people offering various items. If you like the sound of a particular item, you reply to the email and wait to see if you are chosen to receive this free bonus to your business.

The selection process is not scientific: the Freecycler decides who will benefit from the item based on either your speed of reply (were you the first to ask for it?) or the best story for how you will put the item to use (do you *really* need it?). Once you've been informed by your fellow Freecycler that the item is yours, you arrange to go and pick it up. There you are: a new computer, perhaps a shredder for the office or even a beanbag.

There's an eclectic array of amazing artifacts on offer. However, if what you need is not currently available, you can post a wanted email asking if anyone has it. Asking for a particular item really works and prompts people to empty their attics at the weekend.

I believe it is important to donate as well as receive, so make sure you reciprocate and offer the things you no longer need so that someone else can have the chance to put them to good use.

The basic rules of community sharing on Freecycle are:

→ Keep offerings on the straight and narrow. Items you offer must be legal, safe and appropriate for all ages.
→ Don't offer money for something that's being given to you. Offering money takes the "free" out of Freecycling and is at odds with the idea of sharing products for the greater good of the planet.
→ Limit posts to descriptions of the article being traded. Just the facts, please, but do include all the pertinent details.

➝ Keep discussions on topic: no politics, religion or chatter.

➝ If you're unsure about the appropriateness of any listing (such as pets, allowed in some groups but not others), ask a moderator first.

➝ How you respond to requests is up to you. While many offerers follow a first-come-first-served principle, the choice is normally yours. Some like to wait and see if a local non-profit group asks for the item. Many like to wait at least 24 hours, to give members ample time to respond.

➝ Safety first! Exercise caution when divulging personal information and meeting strangers.

(Provided from Freecycle, www.freecycle.org.uk)

My personal experience of Freecycle has been fantastic. Surprisingly, my office does not have the look of an old curiosity shop, with mismatched clutter stacked against the walls. Most of the items fit and work well in the space I have set aside for my daily work.

Here's a list of items I was very kindly given for free during the start-up phase of my company and some more recent additions to the office and my home:

➝ Office tables × 2

➝ Office chairs × 2

➝ Kneeling chair

➝ Laptop (six years old and working perfectly with Ubuntu; see Chapter 3)

➝ Desktop computer (three years old and working perfectly with Xubuntu; see free software)

➝ Colour printer (including colour ink refills)

→ Beanbag for the office (double sized; I ran out of room and Freecycled it again for some other lucky person to make use of)
→ Shelf units × 3
→ Cupboards × 2 (one flat packed and unused from IKEA)
→ DVD players × 4 (lounge, den, garage, office)
→ Televisions × 4 (lounge, den, garage, office)
→ Freeview digital set top box × 2
→ *Linux for Dummies*
→ Printer paper × 23 reams, new
→ Recycled printer paper × too many to count

You may wonder about the DVD player and television in the garage, but I have a bicycle (from Freecycle) that I hooked up to a turbo trainer (from Freecycle) set up in the garage, so that when the weather is at its worst I can catch up on a few DVDs (from Freecycle) and the news while getting some exercise.

One tip is to make your first request on Freecycle for a wheelbarrow. As most members are local, future collections will be local and you'll no longer have to drive to get your free stuff—therefore saving money and exercising at the same time. All it takes is a little effort really.

An alternative to Freecycle is to ask local businesses if they are having a clear out or if they no longer need any items that you might be able to put to good use. This is what the rag and bone men used to do: take the junk people didn't want and turn a profit from recycling it or selling it on. They made a business from other people's junk.

Declutter Expert

If you like sorting through other people's stuff, then get out there and offer your services as a professional declutter expert. Everyone has clutter and stuff that they're keeping for a rainy day. Find friends who don't think they have the time to sort through their own stuff and offer to help them clear it out. Instead of throwing the stuff away, sell it on eBay and share the profits with your client. A bonus for nosy parkers is that you get to rifle through other people's belongings!

Another way to get your hands on the bits and pieces you need to run your business is to ask to borrow it. The lenders may not want anything in return, but you could offer your services and do some work for them for free, leave a voucher for a certain number of hours' worth of your services, or use the tools on another job that pays money and share that with them. Most people's garages and sheds are full of tools that are used infrequently if at all. How many floor sanders are left in people's sheds? How often are drills actually used in a year? People are usually willing to help out and you can repay them in some way later.

Freeq 1 office desk, 2 office chairs, 1 filing cabinet, 1 wastebasket, 1 light bulb: **£500**.

Food for thought

There's a difference between starting a business for free and never paying for anything again. Nevertheless, I want to hand a bit of time over to the Freegans, otherwise known as "waste reclamation experts."

Although Freeganism sounds like it's from another planet, it's actually a very worthwhile pursuit. Freegans aim to ditch conventional economic constraints through finding free alternatives for all their daily needs by community sharing (as we have discussed), foraging for food and other bits and pieces, and working on the basis that we can all live our lives in a civilized yet free economy. I like the way they are thinking already. You can find out more at http://freegan.org.uk.

It should be noted that Freegans live an anti-consumerist lifestyle and may choose to forage food for political reasons rather than necessity. The press have famously homed in on Freegans' style of "dumpster diving," literally picking up and using discarded food from restaurants and goods from supermarkets that have spoiled packaging or are about to go out of date. In general, the food is safe and is often of a high quality.

A little research into the movement shows some excellent tips for anyone wanting to start their own business:

→ People throw away perfectly good products—find them and use them to your advantage.
→ Don't worry what people think about the way you behave, it's your choice.

➡ Finding alternatives is not that difficult.

➡ Barter with what you have spare to get what you require.

So take your lead from the Freeganist movement and have a look around for alternatives. Why not hang around the back of a supermarket one lunchtime and see what you can pick up for free. Is there such a thing as a free lunch? In this case I think so.

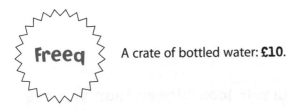

Freeq   A crate of bottled water: **£10**.

Business cards

Business cards are a good idea so you can easily tell other people who you are. If you want a set for free, visit Vistaprint (www.vistaprint.co.uk). You will have to pay the postage and packing, but the cards and all sorts of other bits and pieces for your business are free—T-shirts, postcards, rubber stamps and other things you've probably never even thought of.

Why does Vistaprint do this? The reason is simple: if it provides you with free stuff now, who are you going to get your paid stuff from when the time is right? This is called excellent customer service in the highly competitive design and printing market. You don't have to go back to Vistaprint, but the company did help you out when you needed them to, so follow the freesourcing ethic and invite them to tender for your next piece of business. Suppliers value customers and customers should always value good suppliers.

 250 business cards: **£50**.

Making yourself look bigger than you are

If you put in place all the ideas mentioned in this book to make your business look bigger than it actually is, you gain credibility points out there in the business world. Encourage your customers or suppliers to believe you are a large, well-established organization from what they see in the press, read on your website and how you act professionally. Don't give them a reason to question the degree of risk associated with doing business with you. You are your business, so make sure the business seems as big and believable as suits your marketing plans.

Using all these ideas, I was able to make it seem from a distance as if I was running an established European-headquartered pharmaceutical organization with at least 300 people involved in the day-to-day running of this well-oiled machine.

Paul Davidson Shortlist Me Recruitment

With a wealth of knowledge and contacts in the financial services market, Paul decided to set up his own recruitment business. It had always been drilled into him that turnover was vanity and profit was sanity, so with that in mind he set about keeping costs to a bare minimum. The problem he faced was not having the start-up revenue to get established.

He found an office and negotiated a three-month rent-free period. He contacted various stationery suppliers and eventually find a local firm who agreed 90-day payment terms for a slightly increased per item price. Paul had to pay for phones to be installed by a recognized supplier, but when its installers failed to show up on two separate occasions, it had breached its customer code and, after a compensation claim, Paul was offered £8000.

He recruited two other consultants on a commission-only basis, who were in no doubt that their role was to fill positions. In return, they would receive 50% of the fee after costs, payable on payment of the invoice by the client. All candidates were sourced by direct headhunting or using free candidate recruitment sites, so there were no marketing or advertising overheads. Paul's company now has a turnover of nearly £1m.

Some people call this using smoke and mirrors, employing creative trickery to mould a certain personality in order to do business. As long as you're professional and do the job, what's the problem? But remember, don't fool *yourself* into believing you are bigger than you actually are.

freeq Running a multinational business, per day: £5 m.

Protecting your ideas

Ideas are worth money. If you want to sell your ideas, you will have to prove that you own them. To do this you will need to learn a little bit about patents and trademarking.

Trademarks and patents

All the information you need is available on the website of the UK's Intellectual Property Office (UKIPO; www.ipo.gov.uk). Become an expert by reading and learning what needs to be done. Trademarking and patenting are part of a process—learn how to do it.

A trademark is symbol that is distinctive of your goods and services, such as the words you use in your company name or a picture logo representing your brand. Having a registered trademark means that you can prevent other people using it, although you can license others to use it if you wish. A trademark needs to be renewed every 10 years.

A patent is a set of exclusive rights granted by the UKIPO to an inventor. These rights are time limited and are granted in exchange for disclosing the workings of the invention. Typically, a patent application must include one or more claims that the item is new, inventive and ultimately useful.

Take advice from UKIPO and your local Business Link (www. businesslink.gov.uk) to ensure that you understand the differences between patents and trademarks and how they affect your business interests.

You should be able to do the legal work yourself, although ask for a professional's time to look over the paperwork before submitting it to the UKIPO. When you carry out a bit of DIY trademarking or patent work, you do have to pay for the privilege of owning your own intellectual property. However, once you have submitted the correct forms you can defer payment for up to 90 days.

What is most important is to get to the registry as quick as you can to prove that you have had the great idea first. Sending yourself an unopened copy of your idea in the post and trusting the date is correct on the postmark is not good enough! You need to fill in the right forms, conduct a thorough search to check that no one else has the patent or trademark, and get the stamp of approval from the UKIPO. If you leave it too late, then once the idea is in the public domain you have lost the fight and anyone can build on it.

Copyright

Copyright gives the creator of an original work exclusive rights to it for a certain period, after which it enters the public domain. Copyright generally applies to any expressible form of an idea or information in a written or recorded format. There are very few assets that are uncopyrightable.

To give you an idea of the power of copyright, in 1990 a company named Warner Chappel bought the company that owned the copyright to a little ditty called "Happy Birthday." It paid $15m for the company and at the time the value of the copyright on the song was estimated to be $5m. The copyright on "Happy Birthday" is not due to expire until 2030 and all unauthorized performances of the song are technically illegal unless royalties are paid to Warner Chappel. You tell that to 5-year-old Patrick on his special day. Warner Chappel reportedly earns £1m every year from the royalties generated from the song.

Creative Commons

Creative Commons is a non-profit corporation dedicated to making it easier for people to share their own work and build on the work of others, consistent with the international rules of copyright. The Creative Commons website (www.creative-commons.org.uk) provides free licences and other legal tools to tag creative work with whatever freedom the creator of the item wants it to carry. This then means that others can share, remix or use commercially a particular item.

(sourced from the Creative Commons website, www.creativecommons.org/about)

Digital download store

Start a website that hosts downloadable content, including podcasts, ebooks, audio books, films, pictures and clipart. You need to check that the free content is distributed under a public domain licence, such as a Creative Commons licence. Search the Creative Commons website at http://search.creativecommons.org and add selected items to your portfolio of commercial digital assets.

Your website could be a blog for designers, showing them how to use the products you are hosting, or act as a central point for a specific type of download such as local history content for a geographical location. Subject specialization is certainly a great way to ensure that you have a loyal market. Choose a subject that you are interested in and make sure the stock you have for download is relevant.

You can also sell ad space on the website with Google AdSense (see Chapter 3) to make money from your growing visitor count.

Getting your head around the public domain

The public domain is a range of abstract materials, commonly referred to as intellectual property (IP), which is not owned or controlled by anyone at all. These materials are therefore "public property" and available for anyone to use for any purpose, including commercial and business use. Under modern law, most original works of art, literature, music and so on are immediately covered by copyright from the time of their creation for a limited period of time. When the copyright expires, the work enters the public domain.

Classical music is often cited as a good example of this. Music that has been in the public domain for over 70 years and has not been passed down to family members or had the copyright placed in a family trust is classed as public domain. A website that has benefited from offering open source classical music is Musopen (www.musopen.com), which purports to "set music free."

When compiling a mood board of ideas and selecting free fonts and pictures, even designs to modify, check what is already in the public domain. There is a vast library of stock photos, designs, fonts and graphics in the public domain for you to download and use.

Freeq Fee for a professional trademark lawyer to process some forms for you: **£500**.

Trial business services

There are hundreds of business services on the Internet offering free trials. All you need to do in most cases is submit your details and card payment option. For example, Experian (www.experian.co.uk), a credit check service, asks you to sign up with all your credit card details and then you are able to access your personal financial history. Just make sure that you cancel the service on the right day at the end of the free trial, to ensure that no card payments can go through. You can do this more than once and therefore get the service for free as and when you need it.

Free trials should not be confused with freemium services, which offer cut-down services for free in the expectation that as your business grows and you need the extra upgrades, you will be willing to shell out for the premium, paid-for service. There is a whole host of freemium services on the Internet, not just 30-day free trials but free restricted services, provided by a supplier to entice you into the technology or service. I suggest you take advantage of them, as they are really very good. The business model has been built through heavy competition for your custom. If there are two Internet telephony companies, one that offers a free introductory service and one that does not, which are you more likely to try?

The freemium model also encourages viral propagation. If you like it and want to use it, then you'll tell your network and encourage them to use it, thus getting the technology into more and more people's hands for trial and possible sign-up to the premium services.

 Personal credit check: **£20.**

Banking

You are in business to make money. When it comes to looking after your money, there really is no safer place than a bank. Make sure you find a suitable bank account that gives you a decent rate of interest, but allows you to make quick transactions along with a flexible overdraft facility when necessary.

Most banks would love to have your business and welcome you pouring loads of funds into your account, so they offer free business banking for 18 months or so. The banks do understand that most businesses will not manage to survive the first year of trading and even fewer survive for three years, so the offer is a genuinely good one; they make their money back on everyone else's accounts.

Arrange meetings with a selection of banks in your area. See each one and find out what they have to offer in terms of future services you may require and business advice for start-ups. Any bank has had many start-ups through the door and can give fairly detailed that is relevant to your business.

It is in a bank's interest for you to succeed, so it will have a vast amount of material available for you as a business owner. It is normal for a bank to provide the following toolkits as standard:

→ Business planning tools
→ Presentations from experts
→ Cash-flow forecast templates
→ Profit and loss templates
→ Start-up advice
→ Local business networking

Ensure you are prepared before you see the bank. Make sure you have an elevator pitch prepared and the solid foundations of a top-notch business plan. You may be a possible customer, but money is a serious business and you may have to sell yourself to the bank to get the best deal. You need to have a close relationship with your bank over what could be a long period, so keep in touch.

Minimum 10p processing fee per transaction × 2000 transactions = **£200**.

This whole chapter has been about setting up the foundations of your business. By making sure you have everything in place, you can drive the business forward to meet your goals. You will also by now be far ahead of those who have spent their life savings on getting to the same stage as you.

Think of it like buying a house. It's great to have a big house with a massive garden in a quiet street, but do you need it? You don't want to end up with a shiny big house in Overpriced Crescent that has a massive mortgage against it and is starting to look a little shabby on the inside. Get what you need, not what you want, and learn to do the same with your business.

You can dress the business up to look great, but underneath it may just be you. Your customers and prospects don't know that. Work on your business from the inside out and the healthy heart of the business will keep pumping the cash in.

Total Freeq Value

Circa **£6,000**

(with the £5 m taken out!)

3

IT and Communication

Depending on what type of business you want to start, there are different tools for the job. In any business there is a need for a computer. From communication to marketing and from research to accounting, the computer is a must-have for any size of business.

If you have not used a computer before or believe there is a particular area in which you need to gain skills, then help is at hand. A quick search on the UK Directgov website (www.direct.gov.uk) for "computers" in "Telford" came up with the following:

Search results: 2298 Computers course(s) from 321 provider(s) have been found.

I just used Telford as an example here. My point is that the government wants you to start your own successful business. New businesses are the oils that grease the gears of the economy as a whole. Use the freesources that are available to you to plug any gaps in your knowledge. Certain restrictions apply on many government-maintained websites, so make sure you are eligible.

Also have a look for Business Link free courses and those offered by banks and local business networks. People want to help you get started, as if you are successful you just might be able to help them be successful as well.

If there are some very specific skills you require, think about how you can skill-share or barter your knowledge to ask someone with the skills to sit down with you and help you understand the issue you have.

In this chapter I also look at communication, as most of it is IT based these days and the two fit rather nicely together.

Excellent communication is the foundation of business success. The ability to be in touch and be connected to your client base 24 hours a day is now essential for any size of organization. Now more than ever, there are hundreds of different services for communicating efficiently, based around the various technologies available:

- → Landline telephone (BT, TalkTalk etc.)
- → Mobile phone (O2, Virgin, Tesco, Vodafone, Orange etc.)
- → Voice over IP (VOIP) or Internet telephony (Skype, gTalk, iChat etc.)
- → Fax
- → SMS text (from mobiles and the web)
- → Status updates (Facebook, Twitter, Ping, LinkedIn etc.)
- → Blogs
- → Forums

→ Websites
→ Email (including the forthcoming Google Wave)

Make sure you manage the information flow from this multitude of technologies well, otherwise you'll face communication overload, which very quickly swamps your business and leads to lost opportunities and angry customers.

Business is just a conversation. It's up to you to decide what the conversation is about.

Computer equipment

So how do you get a free computer? Simple, log onto Freecycle (see Chapter 2) and ask for one. Easy. Well, not that easy in real terms, but I explain more below.

If you are lucky enough to be offered a free computer, then take it there and then—it doesn't matter that is 4, 5 or even 10 years old, it's a computer and someone is offering it to you for free.

I don't want to seem greedy but my advice is actually to try to get your hands on two computers. The first should be a laptop, for portability and use on the go with free wifi, as discussed later. The second could act as a server, connected to the Internet, which sits in your home office to act as a back-up machine and a storage device for all of your really important stuff.

However, if you have been handed a computer whose hard disk has been wiped, it will have no data and therefore no operating system. When you switch on your newly acquired machine, you will just get a blank screen. The operating system is the primary instruction that gets a computer going and runs the interface to other software applications. You might be familiar with the likes of Microsoft Windows or Mac OS X. As a freesourcer you will want to find an alternative operating system that does not cost as much.

Luckily, there are many alternatives to the mainstream operating systems. After you have used one of these systems for about a week, you won't even notice the difference between it and the other, more readily available products.

Operating system alternatives are based around the Open Source movement, which was a pioneer of the freesource ethic. This is primarily a development method for software. The promise of Open Source is better quality, higher reliability, more flexibility, lower cost and an end to predatory vendor lock-in. Think of it this way: Microsoft employs about 50,000 developers and pays them to write code. It then packages and sells this code to you for use with your computer. The Open Source movement has about five million developers all contributing updates, rewrites and better coding for small parts of the overall system. The trick is that they supply these updates out of love and the opportunity to work on a free system that benefits everyone. They don't get paid, so there is no charge for the software. It's beautiful, man!

There are organizations that have been set up to take advantage of the need for software support. They repackage the free systems and give them a brand. They will then give the software away for free and make their money on supporting the system. One of the most successful Open Source software solution providers is Canonical. Founded in 2004, it sponsors the Ubuntu brand of Linux software (www. canonical.com). Ubuntu is constantly bug checked and new releases are issued every six months, without fail. It's interesting to know that the founder of Canonical, Mark Shuttleworth, was also the second ever self-funded space tourist.

Ubuntu itself can be downloaded and burnt to a CD or ordered on a free CD from www.ubuntu.com.

Once you have your disk, bang it into the computer, restart and then install the free software by following all the instructions. In as little as 30 minutes you will have a fully functioning computer with an up-to-date operating system and access to thousands of free applications to help you build your business.

Here is a list of some of the applications that you might like to think of installing so you can enjoy your new computer and grow your business:

→ OpenOffice (wordprocessor, spreadsheet, drawing, database, presentation)
→ GIMP (photo retouching and image manipulation)
→ Inkscape (graphics editor)
→ MySQL (database)
→ Apache (web server)
→ Thunderbird (email client)
→ Firefox (web browser)
→ Planner (project management)
→ Avast (anti-virus)

Desktop publishing

Create a desktop publishing service with the computer equipment you already have and free, Open Source software packages such as GIMP (the GNU Image Manipulation Program), Inkscape and Scribus. Create flyers, posters, letterheads and business card proofs for businesses and individuals. Use free digital design assets from the Creative Commons website (see Chapter 2) to create stunning graphical portfolios for your clients.

There are many, many more applications to download and install for free, which are easily as good as their mainstream counterparts and, in many cases, much better. Don't worry about having to learn a new system, as the interface, windows and everything on the screen are very similar to what you will be used to—stick at it for a while and change your habits. You will have to get used to a different way of working, but isn't that why you wanted to start your own business in the first place?

Have a look at information on the following free operating systems and choose the one that suits you best. They are all based on the Open Source Linux "kernel" (www.linux.org), but when the one you choose is loaded up you won't care what's underneath the bonnet, you'll just be pleased with your new computer system.

→ Debian (http://www.debian.org)
→ Fedora (http://fedoraproject.org)
→ Gentoo (http://www.gentoo.org)

⟶ Kubuntu (http://www.kubuntu.org)

⟶ Linux Mint (http://www.linuxmint.com)

⟶ Mandriva (http://www.mandriva.com)

⟶ OpenSUSE (http://www.opensuse.org)

⟶ Slackware (http://www.slackware.com)

⟶ Ubuntu (http://www.ubuntu.com)

⟶ Xubuntu (http://www.xubuntu.org)

The key here is to choose the distribution that you feel most comfortable with. For further info and an online help tool for choosing the free Linux distribution that suits you, have a look at www.zegeniestudios.net/ldc.

One last bit of good news about Open Source software, which could be the best bit of all: the support for your new operating system and all the software is free! No more pressing 3 to be put through to tech support and waiting for a few hours. All the help you need is on the related forums and if you do have an issue, a quick search will turn the fact up that someone else will have had the problem before you. In some cases it may take a little effort, but you should be able to fix all of your issues yourself. You'll become an Open Source software expert without even thinking about it. Well done computer geek, welcome to my world.

Freeq

A new laptop with a preloaded version of the Windows Vista operating system and Photoshop, Illustrator and Microsoft Office: **£1000**.

Getting on the Internet

In order to get the most from your new computer you will need an Internet connection, which nowadays means one thing: broadband.

At the time of writing, I am certain that there are no fully free broadband providers in the UK. However, this will change in the near future as companies realize that there is a profitable model for providing broadband direct to homes and businesses. After all, didn't Freeserve manage to do this with dial-up connections in the 1990s?

However, there are some solutions that fit with the free-source ethic.

Find a free wifi hotspot

If you have a laptop with a wifi connection, you can take advantage of free wifi "hotspots." MyHotspots (www.myhotspots.co.uk) makes it easy for you to find these. All you need do is enter the name of a town or the first part of a postcode in the search box and hit the "Get Results" button.

This site has a total of over 6500 free hotspots listed! This number is growing every day as more and more people contribute their own locations. Many hotspots are ideal for freesourcers as they are in hotels and cafés, perfect for cracking on with a bit of work while waiting for your next meeting. Check out www.free-hotspot.com too.

Orange mobile

Orange branched out into the broadband market in 2006 with the launch of its "free" broadband for Orange mobile customers. It offers broadband and phone "bundles" (Home Starter on pay monthly only) so that you only pay one bill for your broadband, calls and line rental. Get the details at www.business.orange.co.uk.

FON

Although not completely free, this excellent service warrants a mention. The FON model is beautiful in its simplicity (www.fon.com). You purchase a specialist wifi router direct from FON for about £40. When set up, often in less than 5 minutes, this piece of equipment will split your broadband signal into two separate parts. The first signal is a secure Internet connection that you and only you can use, privately and securely and password protected. The second signal is a secure connection that Foneros, FON community members, can use for free.

After you've set up your router to share in this way, you are entitled to roam the world and share other FON users' networks for free. You can see a map online of other FON users and pick up a free wifi broadband signal almost anywhere in the world, just by sitting outside their house or office. Best of all, you earn money from other people using your connection, so you can make back the initial £40 outlay over a few months. Smart thinking. So smart that BT has teamed up with FON and offered the service to its broadband users in the UK. Get more information at www.btfon.com.

Free dial-up

If it's just an email system and basic web browsing you're after, why would you bother paying for expensive broadband or other premium-rate services when you can dial up a UK ISP (Internet service provider) for (virtually) free. These ISPs provide dial-up connections that are free, with no monthly charges, set-up fees or hidden admin costs, although you do have to pay for the phone call at the lo call rate, which is 3.95p a minute during the day, 1.49p a minute in the evening and 1p a minute at weekends. OK, so it's not as fast as broadband, but if you just want to get online then give it a try. You'll need a modem for this, which you can get from Freecycle. Here are some free UK ISPs:

→ http://www.freeukisp.co.uk
→ http://connect4free.co.uk
→ http://www.ukfreeisp.co.uk
→ http://www.12free.co.uk

Many of these sites also offer you the facility to set up a website, which they will host for free. However, do check out the ISP's Internet traffic upload and download allowances. Most web hosting services still have to fork out for bandwidth, which is the amount of data going to and from your account as people access your web pages and download some of your info to their computers. This costs the ISP money, so it needs to limit its liability by setting a cap on bandwidth usage and charging you if your account goes over this limit.

You may think that won't be a problem—but you could be an overnight success and have millions of people downloading your latest piece of software or the video of your mum riding a camel in Tunisia that Aunty Joan took last year. Many web hosting companies cap usage at 500MB per month, which isn't that much really, so you may be forced to upgrade to a paying account. The good news is that by that time your site should be paying for itself.

Data storage and back-up

Every email, spreadsheet, graphic, invoice or photo you generate for your business needs to be stored and backed up. These are known as your digital assets and are actually contributing a monetary value to your business. There is no point wasting time replicating work that you have already done and lost or are unable to find on your system, so make sure you back up everything you really need.

There are many freemium services available on the Internet that can help get you started with a back-up of your files and ensure you have access to them from any computer, anywhere in the world. Now that to me is a great-value service.

Both Mozy (http://mozy.com) and Dropbox (www. getdropbox.com) offer 2GB storage for free (and more space is awarded if you encourage your social network to sign up as well). They work a little differently, though.

With Mozy, after you download and install the software, you select the files or folders on your computer you want to back up and how often. Mozy works in the background from then on, automatically backing up anything you have changed at the intervals you choose (as long as you are online), to a secure online location that you can access from anywhere.

After an equally brief installation process, Dropbox looks and acts like a normal folder on your computer. Once you add or change something in the folder, it is immediately synchronized over the Internet, if you are connected at the time, and stored securely in an underground bunker in a top-secret, safe location. If you are working offline, then once you get back on the Internet, the synchronization happens while you work. It's all very simple—but then the best ideas always are. A bonus is that you can share these folders with anyone else who may be connected to the web and whom you have given permission to do so. These could be work colleagues collaborating on a project or customers uploading files for you.

Remember that 2GB may not last that long, depending on your business. If you're just backing up documents and spreadsheets then you won't eat up as much space compared to large graphic design and picture files. It might help if you think of data in terms of things that you know: 2GB is roughly 480 songs or 3 data CDs or 2000 medium-quality photos. That's not a lot in data storage terms, so use it wisely.

Another way to back up is to get a spare PC and use this as a server, storing and synchronizing your bulk data, while Dropbox or Mozy stores your most important day-to-day work and acts as an interaction point with your customers.

If the worst happened and you were to lose your data, it would take an awful lot of hard work to get it back again. It cost me £250 to get my hard disk repaired and retrieve some of the data when it happened to me. So take precautions before it's too late. Data loss happens more often than you might imagine.

Losing all your data and having to replace it: immeasurable and sometimes impossible.

Email and website

You can easily join the online community for free with Google Mail (http://mail.google.com), Yahoo! Mail (http://uk.mail.yahoo.com) and a number of other free email systems. It really is very simple to sign up and get going with an email address for free. My advice is to set up two accounts, one for your personal life and one for your business life. I use Google Mail because it has many tools that I can employ for both.

If you want people to find your business on the Internet, creating a web page has become brilliantly simple, and free when you know how. You can even have your own domain name for free, albeit with a little advertising from the service provider thrown in. All the stuff you put on your web page can be syndicated (see more in Chapter 6). Best of all, there is a free advertising system that can help your website actually make money for you while you sleep (in the US this is called monetizing; not a word I tend to use too often!).

There are three kinds of service that will be of interest. The first is for people who have never built a website before, who think FTP is something to do with the *Financial Times* and who want a quick and easy solution. The second way is to create a website from blogging tools, which is a slightly more detailed approach but the end results can be stunning. The third is for the more technically able and, while it isn't difficult to learn, it may take you a long time to create a really good website.

Free and easy service

In order to get a simple website up and running, there is no better place than http://sites.google.com. Here you can create an account, choose a template and paste in text, add a picture and list your services for free. It's just like an online wordprocessor: choose bold to make the text bold, paste to add a picture and so on. This really is entry-level stuff and it's free.

Your website name will be something like http://sites.google.com/funandgames, so people will know it is a Google site—but does this really matter to your business?

Blogging

A blog is a web log: an online diary, a sequence of events or a collection of articles that you publish for the interest of your readership. Free blogging tools include Wordpress (http://wordpress.com) and Blogger (www.blogger.com). These two services provide, for free, all the tools you need.

The aim of a blog is to show the world that you have what it takes for them to do business with you. It's like a shopping window onto your world, so make sure you create a warm and welcoming space for both customers and suppliers alike.

I have detailed the steps for you to get up and running with Blogger as it is simple and you can get online in under three minutes. You can also follow most of the same process with Wordpress, a more comprehensive solution with extra bits and bobs to play around with. Have a look at both and see which one suits you better.

Let's set up your free and productive website in six easy steps with Blogger:

1. Go to http://www.blogger.com.
2. Choose the name of the site (best to base this around your business name).
3. Create a profile.
4. Select a template.
5. Create a post.
6. Visit your newly published blog/website.

Extra steps:

7. Go to Feedburner (http://feedburner.google.com) and learn how to use it to track the hordes of people you

hope are going to subscribe to your blog. You can also get access to statistics and add-ons to make your blog more professional.

8. Sign up for AdSense (http://www.google.com/adsense) and learn how to use it to display ads related to your business and earn money through them.

9. Manage your template to create a professional looking site.

10. Create a new blog post every day.

While writing this section of the book I have been through this process again to remind myself of its simplicity. When doing so I registered the Freesources blog at http://freesourcing.blogspot.com and a website at www.freesources.co.uk—take a look to see what I have done with them so far.

Freestart

Professional blogger

Create a blog (see above) and set it up to use AdSense (www.google.com/adsense). You will have to make sure that the content is readable, regularly updated and relevant to a specific target audience and that they want to keep coming back to your site for more on a regular basis.

The AdSense network rotates a set of adverts on your website based on the content you have written so that they're targeted and relevant to your readership. You get paid a sum of money for every click that originates from your blog and transfers the reader from your site to the advertiser. This model works on a global scale and carries on even when you're asleep. Your blog will have to be very well read to make a serious amount of money, though. Most blogs only generate a few pounds every week, but a blog with a good readership, into the millions, can generate anything up to £120,000 a year, as in the case of Neatorama (www.neatorama.com), a trivia blog reporting on the stranger side of life.

When you have blogged your first 100 articles of 1000 words each, you may well have enough content to contact a publisher about turning the blog into a book, which you can then sell to your existing readership.

You can select other products that readers of your blog can purchase from you and take a percentage of the sale: digital assets, books, CDs and anything else that is relevant from your supply partners. Amazon is very good at this model, using blogs and websites to sell its entire portfolio (for more info go to https://affiliate-program.amazon.co.uk).

There are plenty of free resources for bloggers to help you get started and grow the content on your site. And don't forget to put your web address on your free business card so that people can have instant access to what you have to offer.

Many celebrities and even some products have a blog written on their behalf by professional blog writers. This allows time-poor celebrities to connect with their public and gives the brand a personality that customers can buy into.

Copywriter

If you enjoy writing posts for your blog, register on elance.com as a professional copywriter. Submit a profile full of testimonials, your biography and examples of your work. Bid on a project, win a project, do the work and build your business.

But a word of warning—do not simply copy and paste blog entries from another person's website. Their content is copyright and you would be stealing their thoughts and ideas. This is not what this book is about, it's about pointing you to free stuff that will get you on the road to business success.

A professional copywriter to create and maintain your product blog: **£250** a month.

Technically advanced users

When you are ready to move up a gear, have a look at Drupal (http://drupal.org), Joomla (www.joomla.org) and Wordpress (http://wordpress.org), already discussed above. These are content management systems (a big word for corporate blog engines). All three technologies are free and used by thousands of corporations worldwide as well as millions of individuals to give themselves an edge over standard blog users. However, to use these technologies you will need to register a separate domain name and understand FTP (File Transfer Protocol) technology, which isn't really as geeky as it sounds.

Both x10hosting (http://x10hosting.com) and FreeVirtual-Servers (www.freevirtualservers.com) provide free (and ad-free) hosting solutions for your shiny new website. All you have to provide in return is a small amount of cash as a set-up fee and another small amount to register your domain name (think of a domain name as a web address—the one that starts with www.).

Once you are registered with a host, you can upload one of the free content management systems mentioned above and start to create your top-end website. Although this method is not entirely free, for as little as £15 and taking it slowly, you can have a really solid platform for your business's presence on the Internet and a point of reference for your clients, customers, employees and stakeholders.

Professional template-based website or blog with registration, videos and podcast capability: **£5000**.

Communication

Every business needs to communicate with its customers, but how can you do this for free or for the lowest cost?

Mobile phone

Most of us have a mobile phone these days, and if you sign up for a pay monthly subscription you don't need to pay anything for the phone itself. If you opt to do this, restrict your use of the phone for outgoing calls and texts so that you can choose a very low-cost tariff, at around £10 a month.

But there are other solutions. In order to create a new mobile network, many mobile phone companies offer free SIM cards preloaded with 100 minutes of free calls. They do this to encourage you to add this SIM card to the phone you already have, instead of using your existing pay-as-you-go provider. The issue here is keeping the same phone number, which is important if you've put it on your business cards. If you choose to change providers, just phone your existing network for a free PAC code, which allows you to transfer your number in a couple of days.

Why not get an old phone from Freecycle and get a free SIM card with a business number and just don't make outgoing calls? That way you have a free mobile phone and your customers and prospects can contact you wherever you are. It won't be the latest, greatest gadget in the world, but it will enable you to receive texts and phone calls for free. Just have a hunt around the lesser-known networks for the free SIM card offers.

 **Freeq**   Average cost of a mobile phone: **£103.56**.

SMS

Once you have your mobile, there is a host of tools available for low-cost and free text messaging.

One example of this is CBFSMS, the CardBoardFish Short Message Service (www.cbfsms.com). There are no sign-up forms or registration, as this service is driven by advertising. Just enter your mobile number, the message and your name, and click "Send." You are asked to opt for delivery confirmation and/or replies. Replies allow the person you're texting to reply to your SMS. You can read replies for free online.

Free services such as this, which are advertising driven, can be erratic and not very professional when trying to keep in contact with your customer base to inform them of new products or services. When you can afford it, switch to a more professional service with a mobile service provider, many of which offer free texts every month in any case.

A free application that you can download to your phone is smsBug (www.smsbug.com), which offers you access to a secure, simple, dependable, high-capacity messaging platform. The website offers bulk SMS delivery, address book and group functions, history reporting, bulk imports of contacts and so on. You do need to pay for credits, at €0.03 per credit, but that's only a few pennies really. If you can get one sale or new prospect to contact you, then this might be the lowest-cost sale you've ever made.

For an alternative SMS service, have a look at YoutextR (http://youtextr.com), which offers 300 texts for free over a three-day period. However, this is a subscription service and, unless you cancel your subscription, will bill you at £4.50 a week. Nevertheless, it's a good free start for an SMS campaign to get your business going.

300 texts at an average cost of 6p: **£18**.

Voice Over Internet Protocol (VoIP)

If you have set up your computer correctly then you will have access to more communication tools than you will know what to do with.

One of the simplest to set up is Skype. That is, if you have all the basic equipment. Skype lets you make computer-to-computer calls using its technology for free. All you need with your computer is a microphone and some speakers. If you have a webcam you can make free video calls too. Find out more at www.skype.com.

Skype uses the Freemium business model, offering the most basic services for free in the expectation that once you are hooked on the technology, you will upgrade to the better quality and wider range of services it offers.

Connection and first month's landline telephone line rental for solo start-up business: **£117**.

Status updates

The recent phenomenon of real-time updates to social net-working sites has taken hold internationally as a free resource with which to communicate directly with the people around you in your social and business networks. Just sign up to your preferred social networking site (see Chapter 1 for more on these), add some friends and colleagues and update your status. For friends and family it could be as simple as "on my way to a meeting back at 17:30 make sure the tea is on."

However, think about how you can use these status updates more effectively:

→ 2 for one at mykangaroopouch.com this weekend only—carry your baby safely
→ Free pizza for under 6s at PizzaTheActon, High St, Acton Town Tues & Thurs
→ text free to XXXXX and get a new free Xmas ringtone

The benefit of these systems is that they operate in real time, which means you can communicate right here and now with people who are interested in what you have to offer.

Fax

You need to be in contact with all sorts of businesses at dif-ferent stages of their own business technology lifecycle. With this in mind, it is important to ensure that if a customer or a supplier needs you to utilize their specific type of communication tool, you have the technology available to do so. Many organizations still like sending communications by fax—but never fear, you don't need to buy a fax machine.

You can benefit from sites such as www.freefaxtoemail.net and fax2email.comx-computers.co.za. They offer free fax numbers that deliver a pdf version of the fax sent to you direct to your email inbox. You can use this for receiving all those customers' orders, so buying a fax machine seems a waste of money.

If you find yourself needing to *send* a fax, MyFax (www.myfax.com/free) allows you to send two free faxes a day to almost anywhere in the world.

 Fax machine: £50.

Directory enquiries

Now that you have your communications tools for free, don't get caught out paying over the odds to find out phone numbers to call. You can do this for free too, as long as you know how. Of course, you can go to www.118.com or www.yell.com and search for numbers online, but you may be out on the road or lost somewhere, so a phone service may be a lifeline for finding out the meeting address that you were meant to be presenting at 10 minutes ago.

The Number (0800 118 3733)

To use this service for free you must first register online on www.118.com, so the system can add you to its advertising database (though it often works without registration). Then phone the number above, listen to an advert and answer automated questions to ask for the number you want. It's not going to set your world alight, but it's free.

freedirectoryenquiries (0800 100 100)

The Freedirectoryenquiries business model is rather clever. When you call the service, the voice recognition system will try to retrieve the right number for you. To make it viable, the advert you're played while waiting for your number will relate to the business or service number you've asked for. The system also allows you to connect directly, for free, to the advertiser if you think what's being offered is of benefit. For example, if you ask for the National Rail Enquiries number, you are probably interested in rail travel and so you are played an advert for Eurostar, in the expectation that you will consider Eurostar for your next trip to France.

Average cost of calling a paid-for directory enquiries line: 50p per call.

Webinars

Instead of travelling halfway across the country, the continent or the world to see a prospect and explain your product or service, one of the easiest and most productive free pieces of software available to a start-up is a web conferencing suite. This is a group of free technologies that enable multiperson collaboration with no tie to geography. You never have to leave your desk again and can work with anyone in the world!

Webinar (web seminar) tools like Dimdim (www.dimdim. com) set you up with a platform that each of your prospects can link into so they can hear and see your presentations live on the Internet. Collaboration is facilitated through the use of interactive multi-user whiteboards (like a piece of paper and a pen that everyone can use on the Internet), messaging areas, presentation slide shows and graphical drawing tools to sketch out ideas—all from the comfort of your own desk. The IT industry has been using these tools for years and now they are freely available to everyone.

As Dimdim expresses its purpose:

> *Our mission is to enable web collaboration for everyone. We believe that we can improve the world by providing easy, open and affordable collaboration software that anyone can use.*

I shall be running regular freesourcing seminars on Dimdim, so create an account for yourself and log in to hear what's new.

Freeq

Setting up a seminar for 20 people in a reasonable hotel with food, drinks and amenities, including travel costs: **£500**.

Template documentation

Do you know what a proper invoice looks like? Can you create one on your computer? Do you think that people all over the world have created invoices on their computers before and are willing to share them with you for free? Of course they are.

Have a look at websites that offer free templates and contracts for you to amend and use. This saves time and effort and ensures you have a good starting point for your professional business communications.

Software packages aimed at general office use include a whole host of templates, as well as a link to download more from their website. These are used with spreadsheets, wordprocessing, drawing, presentation and database tools to enable you to create the perfect office from the start. Find these at:

→ OpenOffice—http://templates.services.openoffice.org
→ Microsoft   Office—http://office.microsoft.com/en-us/templates/default.aspx

On the Freesources website (www.freesources.co.uk) I have set up a link to some of the basic elements you might need to get started. These include the following:

→ Non-disclosure agreements (NDAs)
→ Terms and conditions
→ Invoices
→ Letterheads
→ Sales letters

➡ Fax cover sheets
➡ Web templates

Other sites you might like to visit for free business templates specific to your contractual business needs include:

➡ NDAs for Free (http://ndasforfree.com)
➡ Click Docs (http://clickdocs.co.uk/free-legal-documents. htm)

Note that you must have your contract documents checked by a professional or someone you trust with experience of contracts before issuing or signing any legal papers. Contracts are legally binding agreements to which you will have to adhere. See the section on getting free professional help in Chapter 2.

 Fee for legal adviser to create a non-disclosure agreement specific to your needs: **£250**.

Professional business applications

As I've already stressed, when you act like a big company, you will be treated like a big company. Successful corporations pay hundreds of thousands of pounds to benefit from the latest technologies available to help run their businesses. Luckily for freesourcers, the providers also offer freemium services. In many cases these free services are not even cut down but simply restricted to two or three users.

Bear in mind, though, that it is imperative that the data you collect is of premium quality, as a system is only as good as the data that resides in it.

I'll start by describing the applications you might want to use, and then tell you where you can get hold of them.

Customer relationship management (CRM)

Customer relationship management is a fancy name for how you organize your everyday contacts with current and prospective customers. CRM software is used to support this process. Information about customers and customer interactions can be entered, stored and accessed to see where the customer fits into the daily operations of your business. Typical CRM tools can improve the service you provide to customers and enable you to use customer contact information for highly targeted marketing and cross-selling opportunities.

An example might be a gardening business that notes on the CRM system when the customer was last visited and, based on preset rules, the software determines when the customer should next be visited. It sounds simple, but try to manage this with 100+ customers and their details. You can make a note of who has, and who has not, bought special lawn treatments from you, then select everyone who has not bought them from you and deliver a tailored email offer with a discount. It's all about managing the "customer experience."

Sales force automation (SFA)

Sales force automation is the process by which an organization manages its sales process with new and existing customers. SFA tools enable sales professionals to maximize selling opportunities and manage their time effectively by employing a professional approach to sales. SFA may be part of a CRM system, as the two share many components.

Web analytics

Google Analytics is a free website analytics solution that gives you detailed insights into your web traffic (who's visiting your website) and the effectiveness of how you market to them. It has a whole host of easy-to-use features that lets you see and analyse your data to make decisions on how best to set up your website and make money from it.

Expense tracking

You may benefit from specialist tools to store, track and manage the day-to-day expenses of those involved in your business. This helps you stay on top of your detailed cash flow and manage your financial resources more effectively.

Specialist database applications

A generic database such as Base in Open Office or Access in Microsoft Office may be all you need, but there are applications designed for specific industries, regions or products.

Project management

Project management is the planning, organizing and managing of resources to ensure the successful completion of specific project goals and objectives. Online tools can help you work more effectively on a project, particularly if there is more than one person involved. Project management tools enable you to manage the delivery of projects on time and on budget by highlighting the critical path of events that need to be achieved before you can complete each stage of the project.

You can get many of these tools through the open-source route, as previously described. Some of them operate online rather than on your computer. The benefit of this is that you can log in from anywhere to run your business—and the data is securely backed up, so if your ancient PC dies, you know that your most important information will be backed up safely.

To start you off, have a look at Zoho (www.zoho.com), which not only offers a suite of online office tools like Microsoft Office, Open Office or Google Docs, but also provides CRM, expense tracking, project management and many other tools that can be used collaboratively and for free in a start-up environment.

> When working with the Zoho tools I asked the support team to help me create a court booking system for my local squash club. They created a fully functional system to a spec that we discussed and posted it to the Zoho projects forum later that week free of charge. Brilliant.
>
> If you have a specific need that they may be able to address, then just ask them if they can provide it for you for free. They will post it in the projects section and allow anyone to download the tool that you asked for. The benefit is that using their database and user interface tools, you can modify any of their created applications to suit your particular needs.

Like any freemium service, these applications are offered for free in order to get you used to working with them. As you grow and need to add more licensees, it's a simple upgrade to widen your use in the business. In the meantime, make use of these excellent systems and act like a true professional.

freeq Implementation and customization (3–5 concurrent users) of all the above systems: **£50,000** in year 1.

Information technology is an ever-changing landscape populated with brilliant new solutions to everyday challenges and complex business issues. The Internet revolution has taken hold and is now a fundamental tool for getting business done in an efficient, timely and professional manner. Luckily for us, the freemium model means that we can all benefit from the entry-level solution to a particular problem.

Take free products to the edge and subscribe to forums to see how other people are using free services. Some free IT tools are being used for completely different aspects of business than the developers first thought of. Get involved and get more out of what's on offer.

Your job may not require a computer to get the work done and get paid, but you will need IT knowledge for ongoing research, marketing and communication. Make sure that you are ahead of the next big IT change, jump on bandwagons early and learn about new and interesting technologies that can help your business flourish ahead of the competition. Don't wait for the IT revolution to come to you, go out there and find the tools that will help you deliver a more profitable business—your competitors will be doing the same.

Total Freeq Value

Circa **£57,500**

4

Help, Skills and Training

"**A**sk for help" is my favourite, top, number 1 piece of free advice—some of the best free advice I was never given when I was struggling to start up.

When that dark cloud looms overhead and the huge blockage in your path seems unmovable, don't sit back and despair, find a way round it. "How?" I hear you cry. "How can I get past this issue that I have no experience of when my business is suffering and I have no cash to throw at the problem to solve it?"

Let's see if TV game show *Who Wants to be a Millionaire?* (supremely apt for this book!) can give us the answer. This quiz involves you answering a number of questions correctly. You're given four possible answers, but if you don't know the right answer with absolute certainty, what can you do?

1. You can choose to make a strategic guess.
2. You may have an inkling that you know the answer and go 50/50, where two of the wrong answers are taken away, which is a better way of saying that you're guessing.
3. You can decide to ask the audience, who probably don't have a clue either.
4. You can phone a friend.

In all my business dealings where I don't know the answer, I go for option 4. I phone a friend. By friend, I mean someone who might be able to help me with my specific problem at that moment. I have solved hundreds of issues just by picking up the phone and calling someone, even though I may never have met or spoken to them before, and asking them how they solved or would solve this issue.

Ask for help

Successful people like to help people who want to be successful. Call non-competing organizations and just ask them where they get their bottled drinks filled or who their packing specialist is, where they source this component and which company would they recommend that specializes in advertising in the industry. As long as you're not a competitor, I am certain that there will be someone there to help, particularly the higher up into the business you call. If they can't help you then they often refer you to people they know who can—and an introduction by referral is a lot stronger than a simple cold call.

Be professional, have your question ready and detailed, and don't waste the person's time—be succinct, be quick and offer them some gratitude. I started by sending over bottles of wine, but I soon realized that this is not what people require for responding to a simple telephone call asking for their knowledge. What they do want is professional recognition of why you came to them in the first place, something that makes them respond: "Wow, this guy called me today and asked if I could help with his packaging problem because he loved the way we do ours. Flattery and gratitude are two watchwords in this instance.

If you are unable to find anyone to help answer your question, then get in touch with me and I'll help out if I can. Not only have you solved the issue at hand, you have probably extended your network exponentially.

There are other ways to ask for help. Go to online forums—there are thousands of these dedicated to specific niche industries, all packed with contributors looking to help you out in business. As a starting point, have a look at the UK website Enterprise Nation (http://enterprisenation.com) and the US website Entrepreneur (http://entrepreneur.com), which have a multitude of forums aimed at every type, size and shape of business, packed full of people who have been through similar situations and who want to help you. Enterprise Nation advertises itself as a free resource to help you start and grow your business at home. If it's free and people are there to help, then why not give it a go?

If you are unable to find the answer you are looking for on business forums, have a go at finding solutions on self-help sites, which explain how to do almost anything you can think of. Here are some self-help and how-to forums for you to browse through—many are US based and the terminology and legal advice may be different, but the principles are the same:

→ Free Management Library (http://managementhelp. org)
→ eHow (http://www.ehow.com)
→ WonderHowTo (http://www.wonderhowto.com)
→ HowTo (http://www.howto.co.uk)
→ wikiHow (http://www.wikihow.com)
→ How To Do Things (http://www.howtodothings.com)
→ Videojug (http://www.videojug.com)
→ Squidoo (http://www.squidoo.com)
→ HubPages (http://hubpages.com)

Freeq

10 hours solving an issue at **£100** per hour minimum: **£1000**.

Get new skills

The traditional career has ceased to exist and instead, individuals are rising up the corporate ladder by pushing themselves with ever-increasing challenges. No longer do you have the job for life that the working population used to look forward to. A career has become a collection of experiences where new skills in differing industries are used to augment the profitability of your brand as an individual. Whew!

What this means is that the more you do, the more experienced and more rounded a person you become. It all started when people went off travelling for a gap year before going on to university. On their return, when they needed to get a job, their CV included worldwide travel, cultural interaction and international work experience alongside the 2:2 they managed in media studies. The people who went straight to university only had the qualification. Who would you choose?

You are a collection of unique experiences both inside and outside the work environment. Grow these experiences by trying new things and exploring new boundaries. You may never know when they will come in handy. Do you remember how Richard Branson abseiled off the Palms Casino Hotel in Las Vegas to promote the launch of Virgin America? I'm not sure he thought this was a skill he would require when he was starting out in business!

If you would like to learn a new skill for free, then offer to work in a friend's business for a day or even a week at a reduced rate or for free if you can afford it. Take time off your normal work if possible. If this new business is something you really want to do, then you will have to learn new skills and invest the time and effort you require to become an expert in your chosen field. Research and reading are all well and good, but there is no better way to learn than on the job. The idiosyncrasies and nuances that make every job unique have to be experienced to be understood.

Writer Malcolm Gladwell set the bar very high with his book *Outliers*, when he established the standard for what it takes to become an expert in anything—10,000 hours of practice. Your only requirement is to find the resource and motivation to practice, practice, practice until you can be considered an expert. But you probably don't have 10,000 hours, which equates to 6 hours every day (including weekends), 350 days a year for 5 years. You want to start a business for free and grow that business quickly, not hang around for 5 years. So how do you become an expert more quickly?

One company in the US has taken this to a new level with holidays tailored around learning how to do your dream job without risking your current career. You decide what business you would like to start up, visit the VocationVacations website (http://vocationvacations.com) and see what people are offering. You sign up, make your way there and sit in on your mentor while they work and then you have a hands-on go at what they do. Although this isn't free, it does underline what I've been saying all along: if you want new skills, go and work in someone else's business.

Mary was made redundant from a large corporation and was offered redundancy pay as compensation. It wasn't much, one week's salary for every year she had been employed by the company. Instead, she approached the company and asked if it would pay the costs for her to retrain as a florist on a recognized course. Mary had always wanted to be a florist, but it took being made redundant for her to decide to take the plunge.

If you do need to retrain, then look at the payment options that the course you require offers. It may provide one of following options:

→ An interest-free pay-as-you-learn scheme. After a small deposit for enrolment on a particular course, there is a monthly standing order payment. However, you are learning and earning at the same time.

→ A buy-now-pay-later scheme, where your studies are financed by a third party. There will be credit checks but this type of option offers a 12-month interest-free payment holiday. You enrol for free, complete your training, become qualified and generate an income from your new career before any payment is due.

Becoming a professional plumber: **£5600**.

Community skill sharing

When researching for my own like-minded network of free-sourcing individuals, I came across a number of sites purporting to offer free goods and services, which called to mind the sage advice: "If it seems too good to be true, it probably is!" However, the Freeconomy Community (http://justfortheloveofit.org) is as true as true can be when it comes to the freesourcing ethic.

This site is based on the fact that we all have skills, time, hardware and assets to share. All you do is register on the site (membership is of course free) and enter your own personal and detailed skill set. There are various elements of the site that you can join to share a particular asset you may have:

→ Skillshare—Share the skills you have and use others' skills where yours may be lacking.
→ Toolshare—Borrow some tools to get a job done.
→ Spaceshare—Let someone borrow your garage and perhaps an office may be available for your meeting.

Landshare (http://landshare.channel4.com) is another initiative that allows you to share any spare land you have with the community for use as an allotment; or to find land offered by others near you on which you could grow fruit and vegetables and get to eat for (almost) free!

Jamie Goddard Garden Design

Jamie Goddard started his gardening business with no money. A classic freesourcing start-up, he borrowed tools from his parents to do a friend's garden. Jamie had always been passionate about working outdoors and working the landscape into an art form. With no money in his pocket, he let it be known that he was available for work in the local area. Starting with small tidying jobs, he would work hard and provide great customer service to ensure that his reputation grew and referrals came in, making the growth of his client base quick and easy. Before long Jamie was able to buy his own tools and a van. Now Jamie Goddard Garden Design employs six people and creates beautiful gardens.

If you are lucky enough to have someone share their particular skill with you, then you can offer that skill to someone else. As Chinese philosopher Lao Tzu said:

> *Give a man a fish, feed him for a day. Teach a man to fish, feed him for a lifetime.*

However, you must also remember the following from Karl Marx:

> *Give a man a fish, feed him for a day. Teach a man to fish and you ruin a wonderful business opportunity.*

You should learn continually from your business experiences.

Buy your own gardening tools **£250** from a DIY shop.

Find a mentor

Anyone starting in business needs committed advice from someone who has been there, done that. The advice should be ongoing and not simply a short-term helping hand. One way of getting this is to establish a relationship with a mentor.

A business mentor must be someone you respect. This respect may come from their success in business or they may simply be someone you admire for their honesty and integrity. Most importantly, when selecting a business mentor you need to choose someone you can take criticism from.

The mentor's role is to be a rock-steady shoulder to lean on, someone to call on when times are bad and also (very importantly) when times are good. Perhaps the mentor you have chosen is in a similar industry and acts like a board member to your business, finding opportunities and high level referrals. Maybe the mentor is in a different business and can investigate where complementary benefits might be created and cost savings delivered.

When choosing a business mentor, think about the following:

→ Why do I need a mentor?
→ Why would this person want to be involved with me?
→ How can I reward this person for helping me out?
→ Does this mentor have a mutually beneficial network of contacts we can share?
→ Does my mentor have a particular skill that I lack?
→ Can I respect the constructive criticism this person gives me?

Big business board members command astronomical fees for advising companies on strategies and tactics. A mentor gives their time and expertise for free in the expectation that they can help you become a success.

Some consulting organizations will offer to mentor you for free at the early stage of a start-up. In return, they expect to be given a small percentage of the business, commonly known as sweat equity. They provide work for free in return for a part of your organization in the expectation that they will receive a pay-out as the business grows. The sweat equity keeps them interested in the growth of your business and enables you to exploit their network and business knowledge.

Someone who has made a career of mentoring is Colin Glass, a chartered accountant who started his own practice, Winburn Glass Norfolk, in 1975, and who has assisted over 230 start-ups. He is passionately interested in entrepreneurship and recognized a long time ago that charging on a time/cost basis was inappropriate and impractical for small start-ups when they need financial breathing space the most.

Colin has always been prepared to assist budding entrepreneurs by agreeing to postpone fees until the business can afford them. At the same time, he joins the board as a non-executive director and takes a small sweat equity stake in the business, believing that he can add value through his experience, expertise and his vast and ever-expanding contact base.

40 hours of mentoring, business advice and professional help at **£100** per hour: **£4000**.

Motivate yourself

Sometimes we all need a little motivation. Short of employing a PA or a mentor, you can hassle yourself for free using a handy little website called HassleMe (www.hassleme.co.uk). All you do is add a hassle, something that you need to do and you know you won't unless you're continually reminded. There is no log-in, simply write out the hassle, indicate roughly how many days between each email together with your email address, and the system will send you a randomly timed reminder.

I have two hassles set up on the system; one a reminder to write a daily blog entry and the other to do some sport every day. They do seem to be working for me. Here are some examples of other people's hassles:

→ Inhale. Exhale. Do it again. And again. Smile. Live in the present. Have faith in the future. Know that you are on the right path. Remember who you are—roughly every 2 days

→ Be strong. Be beautiful. Go for a walk today no matter what. Take time for you! Love yourself!—roughly every 2 days

→ Follow up with 3 people about my business—roughly every 1 day

You get the idea: create a hassle and do what you are told.

Freeq

Employing a personal assistant: **£28,000** per annum.

Setting up a business from scratch and with no money can be a heart-rending and lonely process. The more you surround yourself with people who have experience of your situation and professionals with in-depth knowledge of your industry and a real interest in what you are trying to achieve, the less alone you will feel.

When I started up, I was in my back bedroom on the end of a phone, and there was no one outside my family who understood what I was up to. I had to expand my network to make sure I had the best chance of success. I urge you to have the guts to ask yourself if you are good enough alone to make this work, and if you have the necessary skills to drive the business forward to a successful conclusion. Loners make good inventors, but they don't generally make good entrepreneurs. Don't be an inventor with a good idea that never made it, be an entrepreneur who uses everything at their disposal to generate a business from nothing.

It's very easy really, so I'll end the chapter by giving you some great free advice: ask for help.

Total Freeq Value

Circa $(42{,}000 - 3500) + 250 =$
£38,750

5

Research, Innovation and Prototypes

Just as there is no reason to sacrifice quality just because you are using freesources, you also shouldn't skimp on the basics of understanding and developing your business. All business ideas require research and innovative thinking, and depending on your industry, you may need to create prototypes of your product or market test your service as well. That's what this chapter is all about.

Research

There is simply no better way of understanding the opportunity for your brilliant idea than to get out into the real world and ask people directly, face to face. It is an absolute necessity that you knuckle down and get on with your research at the very earliest opportunity in the lifecycle of your business.

All entrepreneurs believe that the germ of an idea that has started to grow in the back of their complex mind is a goer and will have a massive following—but how many products end up failing? Let me rephrase that—how many brilliant products end up failing? It's still something like 9 out of 10 in certain industries. Why do you think this happens? Is it because the product itself is a dud? No! It's because the idea was brilliant and groundbreaking, but the research into the commercial opportunity did not drive every last morsel of information into the development of the concept, which might have ensured its success.

Some of the reasons your new business venture may fail include the following:

➙ Companies have vast resources tasked with coming up with new and exciting products. What they should be doing is asking customers what they need rather than asking them to buy what they have created.
➙ If you do down the route of replicating someone else's idea then all you can really compete on is the price. Try to find an unmet quality issue and build the business on that instead.

➥ A weak approach can kill off a new venture before it gains momentum—be bold and start strong.

➥ For a new product to be successful, you need sufficient sales. You would be amazed at the number of companies that design a product for a market that cannot sustain it.

➥ Too many inventors come up with great products but don't have the skills to sell them. Sales drives businesses. Learn how to be a good salesman and grow the business success.

➥ During start up there are thousands of choices to be made whilst creating the product. Which colours to choose, what shape the packaging should be, who the target audience is. Make quick and simple decisions and stick to them instead of tying yourself in knots.

➥ Listen to people but make the decisions yourself. It might be a case of too many cooks spoil the broth. Don't do in unprepared. Make sure you have the confidence built upon solid research and market understanding. Too many ideas are gut feel—get the gut data behind your ideas as well.

Many of these reasons for failure can be solved with research. Ask the market what they need to be solved by the introduction of your new product—and make sure you understand the answer. Without research you will have a very short business career. Maximize sales by offering a well-crafted product or service that your market helped to create.

> I started a company four times. The idea was to create a product that when added to refilled bottles of water would create a vitamin-enhanced and refreshing soft drink on the go. I failed the first three times mainly because I was creating products for myself and not scalable solutions for the mass market—very costly. I thought my idea was brilliant, but I didn't ask the right questions such as how much would you pay for a sachet, where would you look to find these products, how might you use these types of product. I asked questions that I knew the answers to rather than using the research to inform me of things that would help in the progress and growth of the idea.
>
> I am pleased to say that with perseverance and some meaningful research, my product is now being sold all over the UK in the majority of supermarket retail outlets. Wahoo!

Get yourself out and onto the streets. Talk to people who are in your chosen target market for the idea. Check to see if those outside the target market can give you any input into the development of the project. Why should you be the only one who contributes to the progress of your idea? You need to share the research effort with people who can help you.

When I first started my business from home I was really worried about people taking my ideas and paranoid about others being able to have the resources to do them better. Then I saw this quote, which reminded me how conservative most people can be when looking at true innovation:

Don't worry about people stealing your ideas. If your ideas are any good, you'll have to ram them down people's throats.

Howard Aitken

The alternative is to pay professional research organizations such as GfK NOP, Ipsos MORI or Gallup large sums of your precious money to do it on your behalf. I spent £1500 on my initial research and although this backup gave me the right to carry on and the confidence to move ahead, I should have trusted my gut instinct because I turned out to be right—I really wish I had saved that money and spent it on product development. Using a professional organization adds impartiality and credibility for customers and suppliers, but it does cost money.

A word of warning: do not make up your research. You may be tempted to skimp on this process, but you will only be kidding yourself and your investors. Be diligent and create a research plan that is as risk free as possible.

Depending on the scale of your start-up, getting friends and family to go to different towns and ask people direct and relevant questions that you can build into a research document can give you a massive boost that your idea is one worth pursuing. It also proves the proposition for investors, gains a buzz among your target market and gives you a contacts database of interested people's email addresses.

It may be the first time you go out into the big wide world and say the words "I wonder if I could stop you for a moment, I have invented a new XXXX," but it probably won't be the last. Just watch the person's eyes change when they realize that they are speaking with an inventor and an entrepreneur—it's magical and if that doesn't keep you going, nothing will.

How much money does it take to spend a Saturday asking people what they think about the service provided by a potential competitor? It's only going to cost you a sandwich and a bus ticket—but then a true freesourcer would make a packed lunch at home and get a lift into town, so essentially it can be done for free.

Ask your audience, gauge their interest and collate the research into a meaningful document. It's true that people are not always willing to help—especially on a busy Saturday when shoppers just want to pass you by. To get the best out of people you need to engage them in meaningful conversation and not merely stop them on the street for an irrelevant chat. Choose your research prospects carefully to get the best results.

As well as getting out and about, there is a vast array of resources available for free for you online. But some words of warning about online research: there is too much information and not all of it should be used! Billions and billions of web pages are devoted to misinforming you and overcomplicating the research you need to carry out. Quite simply, the amount of information available is too huge to get your head round it all without melting your brain.

Both too much and too little information can be damaging—find the right balance from the numerous authoritative sources. Information on the web may not always be factually correct. Use tools such as Wikipedia (www.wikipedia.org, a free encyclopedia, competitive research tool and learning environment), but make sure that you have a second source confirming the information you find. Websites that are non-political and unbiased should also provide some good information for you, so check out government-run information sources. I have found that the BBC's website (www.bbc.co.uk) is a deep information store with many facts and figures that are true and accurate.

Research consultant

Help companies gather information on their target audience by offering research services. Sit with the client and work out what their motivations for the research are, who the target market is and what data they would like to be collected. Explain the process by which you gather information and how you intend to deliver the results. The survey research can be conducted over the Internet, over the phone or face to face. Choose the medium that best suits you and the project. Remember to claim back expenses such as telephone bills and postage costs when you invoice the client.

Freeq

Using GfK NOP to ask 2 questions to 1000 members of your target audience, then collate and present the results to you: **£1500**.

Generate great ideas

Starting a business in an industry you know and love ensures that you can leverage the insights and the network that you have created thus far over your career. But even after you've started your business, to avoid stagnating you still need to keep coming up with great ideas—or do you?

Many people are continually searching for that killer app or wonderful new concept that will change the way the world turns. This is a difficult task. How often can anyone come up with a new product? Why make it too hard for yourself? You don't need a fantastic idea that no one else has done before, just have a look at what's already out there and do it better.

It may be that the whole concept for a new product already exists and the opportunity for a commercially viable business is available for free. I have talked about the Open Source movement from a computer perspective already, but what about other Open Source products? What about an Open Source recipe for a new cola drink?

OpenCola is a brand of cola drink created by a Canadian software firm to explain the term Open Source. The cola is unique and the company behind it has published the recipe and instructions for how to make it in commercial quantities. It allows you to create, modify and improve on the recipe as long as you in turn license the new variant under the GNU General Public Licence.

Have a look at the Open Source repository for any kind of Open Source product that you can build a business from. For example, Nibbledish (www.nibbledish.com) is an Open Source cookbook.

Freeq — 5 days' food development consultancy at **£1000** per day to develop and test an innovative food product: **£5000**.

Sell what you have

Don't wait around for the production version of your awe-inspiring widget. When you have managed to get a sample, however early a stage it is at, use this as a visual indication that you are ready to trade. Approach customers and prospects with the prototype and get advance orders. By asking your user base for help and advice you gain valuable feedback, and this initial interaction with the prospect starts a relationship. This is particularly valuable when you are selling business to business, not least because you approached them first with the concept and showed them where they could gain an advantage for their business earlier than other companies.

I have seen people make paper and card models of their innovative packaging, held together with sticky tape and paperclips. I have seen the same prototypes in the hands of buyers and then in production on the shelves of the retail giants. As long as people believe that you can carry through with what you are telling them, they will believe that they can trade with it. The better the presentation of the idea, the more real it becomes in people's eyes. This works for investors as well as customers: make an idea tangible and it derisks the proposition for them.

Have a go at learning how to use the Google SketchUp toolkit (http://sketchup.google.com) to model your idea in 3D like a professional. It shouldn't take too long to grasp the basics and there are plenty of tutorials and forums dedicated to helping you get your idea into the digital world. As well as giving you all the tools for free, Google SketchUp has a library of prebuilt models for you to download, some for free and many for a low price.

If Google SketchUp is not detailed enough for you, you can move up to Blender (www.blender.org), a free professional Open Source 3D modelling tool. Blender is used by gaming software companies to create the creatures, vehicles, houses and other bits and bobs that go to make a 3D computer game, so it should be extensive enough to do whatever you need.

These tools are not fully fledged computer-aided design (CAD) tools, but they go about 75% of the way for free, so download them as an economical alternative.

 Professional CAD design package: **£2000**.

A prototype is a very powerful extension of the elevator pitch. By visually and tangibly allowing your customers to see and feel the idea, they are drawn in and can give valuable feedback.

Kangaroo Pouch Baby Slings

Lisa started her business very simply: she came up with an idea for a cheap and effective baby sling that enabled new mums to have both their hands free while keeping the baby close to them during the day. Her baby sling is effectively a single piece of strong and fashionable material, looped and sewn together to form one piece. Lisa approached a local remnant haberdashery shop and asked for offcuts of material that she could practise on before she bought the material she wanted. There was so much material that once her skills had been mastered and the pattern for the sling had been created, there was a vast array of leftovers that she made into saleable items.

Lisa asked her husband if he could help her design a logo around the name she had come up with—Kangaroo Pouch Baby Slings. He in turn asked his design agency if they could do him a favour and design a logo for his wife's new business for free—this they did and an amazing job it was too.

Her husband also designed a website while Lisa created the copy, instructions and details of the product, and the backstory to the business. Another friend was asked to take some photographs for the collection, which were used on the website.

Sales were generated initially by word of mouth and then by Lisa offering to show the product at antenatal and prenatal baby yoga and baby massage sessions at the local leisure centre. This was the perfect target market for this product.

Family members create the product when demand is too high for Lisa to cope on her own and she is now able to afford to buy the materials and packaging she needs to grow the company.

Many software companies choose the prototype route when developing new programs. They release an "alpha" version of the application, which may be full of bugs and lack finesse but still provides a solid solution. There is no payment for the alpha release, but a donation is requested towards keeping the development going. The user chooses how much to donate and if enough people join in the fun, a beta release is created and the users who donated all get to try the application for free. This process continues until the development phase is completed and the application is released—and then carries on through upgrades and enhancements over the lifecycle of the product.

So don't just sit there thinking about your idea, create a prototype and make it real. Use whatever you need to make a physical version if necessary. Also think about making an electronic version of the product if you can. Mock-up packaging and design in a graphics package. People who sell ebooks only from their websites are good at this. They have an electronic book for sale, so they mock up something that looks like a real book, when in fact it has never been near a printer in its life.

Making it real for other people also makes it real for you.

Professional design for a new brand of shoes, including branding, design and product mock-ups: **£8000**.

Get money to turn ideas into products

Getting financial help to turn your idea into a product has historically been very difficult, especially during economic downturns, which are more about saving than investing. In adversity there is nevertheless opportunity.

The Chinese use two brush strokes to write the word "crisis." One brush stroke stands for danger and the other for opportunity. In a crisis, be aware of the danger—but recognize the opportunity.

Regional initiatives funded by the government (via the Department for Business, Innovation and Skills, www.berr. gov.uk) are on the increase. In Yorkshire, for example, the regional development organization Yorkshire Forward is helping start-ups by providing innovation vouchers for companies that reach minimal criteria. The qualification for these vouchers is a single day's trading!

To qualify as having a single day's trading, all you have to do is make a phone call—that's it, you have started trading. Now you are entitled to a £3000 voucher that enables you to go to any Yorkshire-based university or participating academic institution and ask for their help in designing your innovative idea and making it one step closer to being real.

These academics have access to knowledge and facilities far beyond your current reach and they will employ their resources just for you to the tune of £3000. All for a couple of phone calls using the free minutes that come with your monthly mobile contract. It's freesourcing all round!

So what's your idea then? If you're not going to get the voucher, I'll have a go for you. Just go to my website (www. jonathanyates.biz) and send me your elevator pitch.

 Innovation research from design and prototyping specialists at a UK university: **£3000**.

Start a business-to-business software company

When you're looking for innovation you don't have to reinvent the wheel, you just need to see that the wheel is a piece of technology that can be used in other areas that others may not have thought of (cake tin, hoola hoop, inertia storage motor, measuring device, transport device, sundial, cookie dough cutter...) You need to ask yourself: "What else can I do with this wheel?"

The trick is to take some one else's excellent and proven technology and find another use for it. Start your business by evolution rather than revolution.

If I have seen a little further it is by standing on the shoulders of Giants.

Sir Isaac Newton

In the world of IT sales, one of the most commonly held concepts is that of the presale. IT firms employ presales consultants (I was one of them a long time ago) to help sell the product as a technical concept. It is the presales consultant's job to show prospective customers how to solve complex business issues using the technological toolkit they have to offer. Most IT solutions are not out of the box—which means they do not work straight away in your business. The solution will need some adapting to the way a particular business works. In other words, each solution is bespoke. The IT companies know this and so offer the presales consultancy element of the work for free (or at a reduced rate to get early buy-in from the customer). Once the consultancy begins and the solution takes shape, it is difficult to stop the project and start again. Time has been invested and the solution has a timetable to completion.

I know of four companies that approached the IT firms that owned particular toolkits and offered to complete some presales work on their behalf. What they had not told the IT firm was that they had a prospect for this solution in mind already. The toolkit was used to build a prototype and the prototype was sold onto the customer. The clever bit is that to implement the solution the customer would need to go to the owners of the toolkit, which the firm can now provide to them at a commission.

Although the intermediary company doesn't own the intellectual property rights, it can now brand the offering as its own. Now free to sell this technology on to a growing customer base, the newly formed company has not paid for the innovation, has used someone else's tools and has profited from branding the solution for which it had had the idea.

Everyone wins in this situation. The customer wins, because they are getting a true business solution at an affordable cost with professional installation and consultancy. The owner of the toolkit wins, because it gets a licence fee for its technology for every implementation sold. And the intermediary gets the start of a growing organization that specializes in providing bespoke solutions based on the success it has already had in the market with its offerings.

Maybe you could do something similar?

Freeq

Development costs for IT solutions toolkit architecture and bespoke implementation for clients: **£250,000**.

White labelling

Creating products from existing technology or reinventing the use of a particular technology can be a very simple and time efficient way to start and grow an organization. You can get from no company to growth company in 3–6 months using this reinvention option. Watch new technologies as they emerge and think round the edges, apply your own industry knowledge and see where solutions and business advances could benefit from this technology.

Ideas are infectious: make sure yours are worth catching.

This kind of product innovation is called white labelling: taking an existing technology, product or service and, with the permission of the owner and usually under licence, creating your own branding to sell on a product portfolio for yourself.

freestart

White labeller

Manufacture a jar of pesto and sell it on the Internet in bulk, offering a label-design service to buyers who can then sell their own version on to customers. All you need to start up is a few jars of samples and some design software, freely downloaded from the Internet, as well as a quick check that you comply with food safety regulations (see www.food.gov.uk). You could do this with any homemade product, but then so could everyone else. So take a look at branding your own ideas to make your products the choice of the consumer.

Next time you take a sip of a branded diet cola, look at the ingredients. Many soft drinks use artificial sweeteners, a technology used in the product manufacturing process under licence. The technology employed to create these sweeteners has been patented by third-party manufacturers and as such is intellectual property. But why would the soft drinks manufacturers reinvent this already proven technology? Or have a look at the licence on most software packages, which will declare that the company uses integrated technologies in its solutions (after all, isn't that what a package is, a collection of technologies working together?).

Use technology as a set of building blocks, as a playset, as a toolkit. Paint your inventions from a palette of existing technology.

A company in the UK created a new brand of functional vitamin C drink by taking an existing, branded, orange concentrate product bought in bulk from the normal wholesale supply channel. The company then created a new product by emptying all the bottles into an industrial standard mixing machine and adding a specific quantity of vitamin C powder. It rebottled the drink, slapping on its own brand label, and marketed it as a vitamin C enhanced squash concentrate for kids, which sold very well on the Internet.

If you are using other people's technology, then make sure you are adding real value to the proposition and differentiate your product in the market to make it stand out to customers.

Dasani, the top-selling bottled water in the US, took good old British tap water, filtered it to a very high level using reverse osmosis, then rebottled the now enhanced, purer tap water under the Dasani brand. However, the Brits were not duped: they realized that this was just bottled tap water selling for £1 and the brand failed in the UK. However, in the same form it is constantly seen in the top three bestselling US water brands. It's just filtered tap water.

Children are very good at adding value to existing products: selling homemade lemonade, washing cars, selling cookies, odd jobs, taking out the trash and so on. They have no product except their own design and a willingness to be creative. In fact, children have the mental capacity to be amazingly entrepreneurial. They have a vast resource of creativity, no fear of failure and mentors on hand at home. In the main, their ventures are low level, but their creative problem solving is astounding to watch in action.

Product innovation, development of supply chain partners and testing for a new pesto-based retail sauce product: **£15,000**.

Getting stocked up

Of all the many types of business and opportunities mentioned in this book, 80% are service based. What happens if you want to buy and sell a product in order to make your money? How does freesourcing lend itself to getting your hands on some stock?

One way is to ask for old stock from an established business—can you sell time-limited products for a profit?

One of the major problems manufacturers face is timing the arrival of supplies to suit the creation of the products they sell, combined with the orders that their customers require to be fulfilled. In most cases, making more of a product in one go enables the unit price to come down. This is due to the fact that when a machine is running, making stuff, it's doing work that pays for its upkeep (and the capital outlay). If it's idle then it's not making money and is losing value just sitting there. So what many manufacturers do is overproduce to get the cost per unit down and ensure they have enough stock to deliver.

However, in many cases this can cause another problem. Imagine the situation when demand for a product decreases due to better products on the market, really poor weather affects ice-cream sales or when the best before date on food is rapidly approaching. The manufacturer will start to panic and try to offload product as fast as possible, hopefully at cost or just above as an incentive to increase demand from new customers.

As well as food that is about to go out of date, this happens with personal care products like shampoo, soap and washing powder that have had branding and design changes, electronic equipment becoming outdated by new and emerging technologies—in fact, almost anything you can think of.

eBay retailer

If you can source products that are useful and, most importantly, those that sell well, you can set yourself up with an eBay account for free to start trading. Have a big clear-out at home and see if there is anything lying around that you can sell on eBay instead of throwing it out. Ask friends and neighbours if you can sell any items for them and share the profits. You need to make about 100 sales to really understand how best to use eBay and ensure you have enough credibility for people to start doing business with you.

eBay selling is very competitive, so take excellent marketing pictures and use top-notch selling templates to ensure that people buy your product rather than a competitor's. Use the many tips and hints provided by dedicated eBay bloggers to ensure you understand how to make money rather than just sell your stuff.

To ensure a successful freesourcing experience, make sure you receive payment from buyers before outlaying anything to the suppliers of the products, and check that the postage and packing you charge exceeds the actual cost to you.

Use the money you make to create an eBay shop at very cost-effective rates. And expand your success by keeping a database of your customers and emailing them when you have something to cross-sell. Keep customers coming back for more by offering exciting and innovative products.

Manufacturers have millions of cubic feet of product that they either can't get rid of or need to get shot of fast. Some companies specialize in taking this kind of stock and selling it on, but generally they offer really low prices to the manufacturer and sell the goods on very cheaply, as no one wants the cash-flow burden of out-of-date stock.

If you think you can sell what they have, why don't you offer them a buy price for their stock, to be paid 90 days from delivery as is usual in these situations. In fact, you could go for 120 days; they can only say no. Then you have between 90 and 120 days to sell the product. You could even offer a higher price and lower your own margins by offering to buy on sale or return terms, so if you don't sell the goods you can give them back.

Once you have taken delivery of this wholesale stock for free (well, with 90–120 days to pay), you need to get rid of it. Where? How? Who? Panic! Here are a few ideas that I have used successfully:

- ➡ Sell to friends, and if they like the product get them to sell on to other friends who can sell on to other friends. Soon you'll have your own sales force, all wanting to buy your product.
- ➡ eBay is full of great offers and you can undercut the competition with the excellent prices you negotiated with the manufacturer by buying direct from the source. See the nearby Freestart for more.
- ➡ Car boot sales are a possibility. Make sure you pay for the pitch at the end when you have made the money rather than up front, as it then wouldn't be freesourcing. Say to the organizers that you're just having a go and have not done it before, but if you're successful you'll pay a bit extra at the end—I am sure with a bit of

charm and banter you can manage this. I do it all the time.

→ You could also try selling in the street—not the "Oi, mate, I got these watches really cheap" kind of sell, but at a street corner (where local bylaws allow) or on a market stall (use the technique above to avoid hefty pitch prices).

→ See if you can sell it all in one go. Find a company that exports cheap European products to other markets— research customers on the Internet.

→ Sell on to promotion companies that could use the products as free giveaways during a PR stunt.

→ Sell to hotels who might need the type of products you have.

→ Create a group of commission-only sales people to help you sell the product—your margins will suffer, but you could have an exponential increase in sales activity. See Chapter 6.

→ Sell to university students who need more cost-effective alternatives to branded products so they can save all their grant money for other things. You will need to get permission from the university faculty.

If you can't get rid of it all, try and understand why you chose a product that you couldn't sell instead of researching the opportunity to ensure you had a buyer before you bought the stock! Remember, this approach is risky, so do your research in advance and, if at all possible, make sure you have a buyer before you take delivery.

Make sure you understand the product and the market for it in infinitesimal detail, and try to have an outlet to sell to before you buy. Lastly but most importantly, exude credibility by conducting yourself professionally in everything you do, including postsales customer service.

Selling from home

If you enjoy having your friends round for a cup of tea or a glass of wine, some snacks and a natter, home selling could be the one for you. Many companies organize local sales consultants to come over to your house and tell your friends and relatives all about their products. Two notable examples of this are The Pampered Chef (www.pamperedchef.com) and Vie At Home (www.vieathome.com).

You have to provide the people, the place and the party ingredients and the company's representative provides a local sales consultant, expertise with the product, demonstration capability and a host of hints and tips to get the best out of the products. Anything the consultant sells, you get a commission for. The more they make, the more you earn. You might even want to take this a step further and become a local sales consultant, so you're the one giving the demonstrations.

Or, how about taking the rudiments of this business model, finding a product that you can easily get hold of and starting your own home selling business by getting your friends round and selling to them?

When you have sold all the stock—and believe me this can be very hard work indeed—take a break and marvel at the fact that you now have money in the bank by selling free stock. But always remember that 90- or 120-day payment term and don't splash out on a new Maserati. Instead, keep enough back to pay the manufacturer, get cheaper stock next time by paying a portion up front and invest the rest in a marketing or a sales campaign so that you can then sell the stock more quickly and make the returns faster as well.

There may be an issue with many suppliers: if you are a new customer and have little credit history with other suppliers, then how can you prove that you are going to conduct your business in a professional fashion? How do you create the credibility to enable to you to effectively get the product for free and sell it before you buy it? Many suppliers will ask for an up-front payment for a first order. You will need to use all the guile you've amassed by reading this book to negotiate payment terms with a new supplier. Ask yourself why they should trust you with their stock.

iStockphoto.com is a digital photography, illustration and video downloading website. It is a portal onto a wide variety of downloadable digital assets that you can use for business. The photography is provided by you and me, people who need a platform to distribute their work and get paid for it. The copyright belongs to the originator of the product, the photographer or illustrator. iStockphoto simply offers a search, download and payment portal to connect people who need to download stock photography with people who would like to sell a licence to use their photograph. iStock doesn't own the product, it is a conduit for transactions between buyer and seller. Its speciality is providing a service to designers offering a readily available stock of high-quality illustrations and designs for a small amount of money.

 Up-front payment for stock as a new account: **£5000**.

Having an idea is not the difficult part of setting up a business. Even setting up a business is not the hardest part of getting going. Anyone can say they have a great idea and that they have the business cards for their new website to prove it. What is lacking is the hard work needed to prove to yourself and others that the idea is a great one and is worth ploughing on with.

Research is fundamental to innovation, and innovation is fundamental to business success. Without innovation and reinvention you may have a great business that lacks longevity. You have to remodel and refocus your creativity to ensure that you compete effectively in anything you do. If you keep doing the same things, you keep getting the same results. Creative change and speed to market are key for the successful entrepreneur. Create change, be disruptive and make waves in your chosen field.

Total Freeq Value

Circa   **£285,500**

6

Customers, Brands, Marketing and Sales

Ensure that you take every step to gain credibility and build trust in your business. Don't put up barriers to your success and make doing business with you as easy and enjoyable as possible. This chapter will show you that you don't need to pay big money out to designers and branding geniuses for fancy logo ideas to help sell your business to your customers. Instead, what you must do is understand what your organization is and where it is going. You have to be just ahead of the wave and become an organization that people want to do business with.

There are many online resources that can help you create a great brand and even more forums where you can ask people for comments on your brand identity. Use these to grow your brand and your business and create an identity for your customers and suppliers to associate with.

Create your own brand

In order to differentiate your business from the rest of the market, you need to create a unique identity: a set of designs that quickly and easily portrays your values and services to a potential customer while installing trust and good customer service to the customers you already have. Wow! That doesn't sound easy! It would be quicker and easier to get a professional to design a logo and brand artwork for you, but that's expensive and not half as much fun as doing it yourself.

Check out what other organizations have done to create memorable, longlasting logos and, more importantly, how they have kept them up to date.

Make a storyboard of current logo trends, find similar fonts to use and create a store of pictures and designs that best represent your brand's ideology. This is known as a mood board.

Take all the best bits from your mood board and have a go at sketching your own logo. Then send it to a designer friend and ask them to tweak it to give it a more professional look. If you don't have any network contacts in the design world, why not submit it to a design forum to see what feedback you can get on the useability of your design. After all, researching a brand is just as important as researching your product or service. Ask questions such as: "What are the first three words that pop into your head when you see this logo?" Refine the idea and keep the design up to date.

As I practice what I preach, I used GIMP, a very good, if not better, alternative to Adobe Photoshop, to create the Freesources logo on the website http://freesources.co.uk.

Here are a few links to some excellent tutorials and resources on the web:

- ➡ LogoMaker (http://www.logomaker.com)
- ➡ Cool Text (http://cooltext.com)
- ➡ GIMP tutorials (http://www.gimp.org/tutorials and http://gimp-tutorials.net)
- ➡ 1001 Free Fonts (http://www.1001freefonts.com)
- ➡ Dafont.com (http://www.dafont.com)
- ➡ Stock.XCHNG (http://www.sxc.hu)
- ➡ Blue Blots (http://blueblots.com)

Many printers will offer advice on the subject of logos. Contact them and say that you are looking for a print supplier but you are worried about the design you have. Nine times out of ten they will offer to have a look at the logo and get one of their in-house designers to redesign what you have, in the expectation that you will place an order with them for letterheads and business cards.

Remember that everything created by you or anyone else (even if it is on your behalf) has an immediate copyright owned by the person who created it. With this in mind, make sure that you get the rights to the design or the photo you have asked your friends for in writing. A brand is worth very little at the start-up phase but can be worth a huge amount after a few years of growth.

> Carolyn Davidson, who designed the Nike swoosh, was paid $35 for the privilege. In 1971 Davidson submitted the bill for her work after charging the mighty sum of $2 per hour for her time spent on the design. In 1983 Phil Knight, the co-founder of Nike, gave Davidson a diamond Swoosh ring and an envelope filled with Nike stock as a thank-you.

Freeq

Logo design from established local design house: **£2000**.

Find customers

OK, so you've had a great idea, set up a business, got your workspace sorted and now you have a magnificent logo and brand. But do you have any customers? A business without customers is not a business.

One of the hardest skills to acquire is the ability to sell. Although in the US a sales person is a respected professional who provides an essential function to the business, in the UK selling is almost a dirty word. But having a great product or service that you are sure many people will need isn't good enough. You have to be a great sales person to find prospects and convert them to paying customers, then ensure an ongoing relationship with aftersales service and ongoing repurchase opportunities. Customers won't find you or your website just because you have started a business.

Avon calling

After becoming a customer of a local Avon representative, Sharon enjoyed the meetings and new products that her rep brought every week. After about a year, the rep decided to change career and before she left mentioned this to Sharon, who then asked where she would get her products from. The rep was not sure, as there was no one taking over her customers. With 50 regular clients, this was a nice little business that could be operated from home alongside another job. Sharon organized a flexible work timetable with her employer so that she could come to work early and leave late, working four days a week instead of the normal five. Sharon picked up the 50 clients and for no initial outlay obtained a business that was already up and running, selling beauty products from home and the local area.

Create a plan from all the research you have done, draw up a checklist of your ideal customer, and make sure you can find them. If you sell business to business then make sure you select the right people to approach. Don't waste time on irrelevant communication. Build a picture of your ideal customer as a person or of the relevant department in your target business.

Big businesses use proven sales processes to find and engage potential customers. You can use sales tools such as those on Zoho (www.zoho.com; see Chapter 3) to help you hone your selling opportunities, store customer details and manage the regularity and frequency of your contact with them.

If you sell business to business, find customers using your local *Yellow Pages*: it's delivered for free and lists companies in your local area. If you are a design consultancy, for example, phone up a company and say that you saw their advert and have a good idea for them to enhance their branding.

Another way to find customers is to attend meetings and seminars that your prospects might attend. This way you can meet them on informal ground and get to know them rather than cold calling them. Watch out for events that may bring your target audience together.

When Innocent Drinks started up, its founders attended festivals and offered people their new brand of smoothies. They asked people to put the empty bottle in one of two bins. One bin was for "yes I really liked it" and the other was for "no I didn't like it." The "yes" bins were overflowing! As well as market research, they created a great piece of PR and engaged a huge number of potential customers.

Give away free products or services, or get an article in the local paper offering a free two-hour business consultation, or prove to people in a workshop the benefits of being part of your customer base. The free giveaway doesn't have to be a product, it could be a newsletter packed full of information. By doing this you are engaging with your potential customers.

Use your personal network, your friends, your friends' friends, past colleagues, your neighbours. Create a database of prospects to contact—then contact them.

Have a close look at the competition, find out how and why they are contacting customers and replicate their success. When you can mimic the attitudes and ideas of your most successful business competitors and the companies you admire, then you too will become successful.

Richard wanted to be the very best telesales account executive. He made sure he sat next to the winner of the sales person of the month award. He did a lot of seat shuffling, but by the end of the first year, after sitting next to no fewer than seven winners (some who won multiple times), Richard became the sales person of the month for eight consecutive months. What had he done? He had taken the best ideas and worked hard to create his own success from those around him.

Also ask for feedback from people who *don't* want to use your product or service. Sometimes it is more important to find out why they won't purchase instead of why they did purchase from you. You might be able to hone your offering, understand more about the market and convert more of your prospects into sales more often.

You could always save yourself the time, effort and trouble of creating your own prospect database by buying in names, addresses, telephone numbers and emails. But this can cost you dearly. The mailing lists provided by specialist list brokers are vetted, up to date and targeted and for this they charge you money, sometimes a great deal of money.

Instead, you need to create your own list of prospects—a database that is equally vetted, up to date and targeted. In this way you will know who you have contacted, why you contacted them and when to contact them again. And aside from your time, it's free! Best of all, a database is an asset of your business. When it comes to sell the business, the database of names and addresses of your customers and prospects is worth money.

There are strict rules on buying, selling and trading private customer details, so ensure that you understand these rules before transferring the rights to your own database.

Targeted mailing list of 100 names, addresses, email addresses and telephone numbers of ABC1, healthy lifestyle, non-smoking females who ride motorcycles in West Hampstead and who have bought gherkins in the last 12 months: **£900**.

Here are some other free ideas for finding prospects:

→ London Olympics Business Network (http://London2012.com/get-involved/business-network)
→ Local newspaper classifieds.
→ Business stories in the national press.
→ Trade press.
→ Local business networks.
→ craigslist (http://www.craigslist.co.uk)
→ Yellow Pages/Yell.com
→ 118.com
→ Companies House (http://www.companieshouse.gov.uk)
→ Business Link (http://www.businesslink.gov.uk)
→ Department for Business, Innovation and Skills (http://www.berr.gov.uk)
→ Business Network Online (http://thebusinessnetworkonline.com)
→ Find your nearest sales agents for home-based businesses like The Pampered Chef, Vie At Home and Avon, then swap prospects and customer details. After all, they want to find more customers too.
→ Ask a prospect for two names of other people who they think might be interested in your products.
→ Relevant forums for your product. Engage with people who are moaning about a connected problem, which you can then solve for them.
→ The local library (yes, it's not the Internet, but it's still there).
→ The pub (chatting to others can be very lucrative).

A note about cold calling. First, what you're doing shouldn't really be cold calling, you should be calling highly targeted prospects who you already know have an inherent need for your products. That said, cold calling is all about practice and knowing which hot buttons to press while chatting away in order to keep a prospect on the phone long enough to set a meeting date (or sell them a product). This comes with experience, so test out your methods on friends and family. Become a cold calling expert and you'll never be cold calling again.

Freestart

Sales agent

Subscribe for free to *AgentBase* magazine, then, after flicking through the pages, find a product or service you think will be successful and approach the advertiser. The advertiser will want to meet you to discuss whether you are the right candidate and ask you to sign a contractual agreement. Read this carefully, as it lays out the framework of your working relationship.

Take delivery of your first consignment of products and sell them. The growth pathway for this start-up is to create a growing customer base with whom you have a good relationship. Visit them often, even if you have nothing to sell at that time. Find other products that your clients need and offer them as part of a growing portfolio.

Many large companies use this sales model out in the field instead of employing sales people themselves. Choosing the right product is vital to your business success.

Finding customers is exactly the same process as finding a new job:

→ You have skills that you would like to be paid for in return for a period of time in employment.

You have a product or service that you would like to be paid for in return for its provision.

→ You have skills that the employer requires and will pay you for.

You have a product or service that the customer requires and will pay you for.

→ You search out a company that you would like to work for and go through an interview process.

You search out a customer who you think needs your product or service and go through a sales meeting.

→ You market yourself with a history of your achievements to date and show credibility with references.

You market your product or service with a description of its features and benefits and show credibility with testimonials.

→ You work day to day in a job that you have chosen to do to the best of your abilities. All you really need to do is to find the right company to employ your unique services.

You work day to day creating a company that suits your talents. All you really need to do is to find the right customers to buy your unique products or services.

Freeq Employing a sales or distribution agency for your next new consumer retail product on a **£2000** per month retainer and 15% of sales for a year: **£40,000**.

Get publicity

Go through old newspapers and create a database of PR and publicity contacts. Borrow magazines from your friends and flick through them, noting who has written a relevant article and who may be predisposed to writing an article on you or your product idea. Don't limit this to local newspapers and magazines—have a go at the nationals and monthly glossies as well. The higher you aim, the more likely you are to achieve your goals and even above them. Gain credibility by exceeding others' expectations about your aspirations.

Create a nice-looking press release or two tailored to the relevant market and the style of the publication you're targeting. There are many online resources that will help you create a professional press release. To start off with, have a look at www.wikihow.com/Write-a-Press-Release.

In this digital age editors get loads and loads of irrelevant emails sent to them asking to be mentioned in an article. Most are simply ignored. Make sure your release is targeted and relevant to the publication to maximize its opportunity to be published.

Nowadays I would do a big press campaign by creating a highly targeted pack with info and a memorable gimmick or gag. I would send a hard copy rather than an email, because everyone sends emails and they can clog up the system. Do something different and stand out from the crowd.

The last big mail-out I did was to the national newspapers and glossy magazines. We sent them a water bottle with a sticker on the front and a handmade felt superhero-style cape. It was something different and relevant to the product. We attached some product in the pack and sent a note saying "Supercharge your tap water." We received 20 mentions in the national magazines from 80 mailings. This success was mainly due to the editor receiving an empty bottle.

By the way, in true freesource style I managed to get hold of 200 empty plastic bottles by calling in a favour from someone I cycle with every weekend. (Thanks, LGF.)

If you want to save a penny or two on the postage, there are free newswire syndicated websites where you can submit your story via email. These sites will publish your news item to their network of subscribers on your behalf, as well as to Google, Yahoo! and other search engines. I have had some good successes with this method and it's always worth giving it a go because it is, of course, free.

Some sites you may want to visit and sign up to are:

- BizEurope (http://www.bizeurope.com)
- EcommWire (http://ecommwire.com)
- Express Press Release (http://express-press-release.net)
- Free Press Release (http://free-press-release.com)
- Free Press Releases (http://freepressreleases.co.uk)

- Newswire Today (http://www.newswiretoday.com)
- PR.com (http://www.pr.com)
- PR-Inside.com (http://www.pr-inside.com)
- PRZOOM (http://www.przoom.com)
- Press About (http://pressabout.com)
- pressbox (http://pressbox.co.uk)
- Press Method (http://pressmethod.com)

Public relations works on AVE or advertising equivalent. If you get a full-page article, as did I in the *Daily Mirror*, just by calling up and telling them my story, this could be worth between £5000 and £75,000 of advertising. Except—and here is the crunch—someone else has written this about you, and it's not an advert aimed at selling or persuading. This gives your business credibility from a third party.

In the first three months of starting up my business, I managed to get into the *Sunday Times* and the *Yorkshire Post* as well. These were not just mentions, they were half-page articles. I still didn't have a product, but the idea was newsworthy enough. I still quote from these publications as much of the information is as relevant now as it was then.

Never make up quotes about yourself that you can't corroborate with third-party evidence. It can be dangerous to your reputation.

Another good way of getting in the news is by performing a PR stunt of your own design. This is where your creativity comes in. In PR you need to do something different, be creative and stand out. You could create an event in a public place, some kind of stunt to draw attention to your product or service. Simply standing on a train and shouting is not good enough, stand on the train shouting about your product and then hand out a voucher encouraging people to get free samples. Tie the news item in with the product.

Think about a stunt that is relevant to your business, plan it very carefully and let the press know in advance of your whacky intentions. It's important to call both the local and the national press. Who knows, it may be a very slow news day and editors have to fill the papers somehow. Look in the press and see how other companies get in the news—is what they do so hard?

A great and often overlooked way to get some publicity is to enter a competition; a business competition, that is, rather than a wordsearch competition for a mountain bike or a Wii. Many smaller competitions run for the benefit of the sponsoring organization's own PR are undersubscribed.

When I started up my business I won an award within the first three months from a very prestigious food-testing organization. In fact, it turned out that there were only six entrants and the organization invited us all down to their HQ and we all managed to win one of the six newly created categories. Very clever. The organizers managed to get the story into the paper by running the competition; my business plan and marketing materials have the award splashed all over them as proof that the business has achieved an award recognized by an industry leader.

Scour the trade mags and look for competitions that only require a start-up business plan. Tailor your plan for different competitions and see if you can win them. Some of the prizes can be very worthwhile, with office space, computers and even cash on offer. So go for it!

The Million Dollar Homepage

The idea is simple: to try and make $1m (US) by selling 1,000,000 pixels for $1 each. Hence, "The Million Dollar Homepage." The main motivation for doing this is to pay for my degree studies, because I don't like the idea of graduating with a huge student debt. I know people who are paying off student loans 15–20 years after they graduated. Not a nice thought!

So, everyone is welcome to buy my pixels, which are available in 100-pixel "blocks" (each measuring 10 × 10 pixels). You will see the homepage is divided into 10,000 of these 100-pixel blocks (hence there are 1,000,000 pixels in total). The reason for selling them in 100-pixel blocks is because anything smaller would be too small to display anything meaningful.

You can buy as many pixels as you like, as long as there are some available (see the live stats in the top right corner of the page). When you buy some pixels, you can then display an image/ad/logo of your choice in the space you have purchased. You can also have the image click through to your own website. However, no obscene or offensive images are allowed.

The pixels you buy will be displayed on the homepage permanently. The homepage will not change. Using some of the money I make from the site, I guarantee to keep it online for at least 5 years, but hopefully much longer. I want it to become a kind of internet time capsule. So, in the long run, I believe the pixels will offer good value. You will have a piece of internet history!

Reproduced with kind permission of Alex Tew, www.milliondollarhomepage.com.

To see how much press Alex generated for his website, have a look at www.milliondollarhomepage.com/press.php.

If you can come up with a way to get almost the entire population of your country to send you £1 each, you will certainly be on your way to a successful future.

Employing a PR company on a retainer of **£1500** a month for 2 days a week working on your business: **£18,000** annual cost.

If it's publicity and credibility you're after, look no further than Peter Shankman's HARO (Help A Reporter Out) website, www.helpareporter.com. HARO is a daily set of emails that Peter puts together with requests from reporters all over the world who are in need of material, interviews and knowledge on an incredibly diverse and obscure set of topics. The benefit to the reporter, should you decide to help them with a specific article, is that they get to meet their deadline with an excellent piece that you helped them write. The benefit for you is that you could get your name in print in some of the most prestigious publications in the world.

Here is an extract from a recent HARO email. I know it's obscure, but there will have been someone out there with a haircare product who might have been able to boost sales or a local hairdresser who might have wanted to boost the credibility of their business:

Summary: How to create the perfect ponytail
Category: Lifestyle
Title: Editorial Director
Media Outlet: www.beautyxpose.com
Specific Geographic Region: N
Region:
Deadline: 12:06pm EASTERN—22 June
Query:

I am writing an article on how to achieve the perfect ponytail. I am looking for tips or products that can be tested and featured in the article.

Or how about this to help get your idea funded:

Summary: Bootstrapping & VC Stories
Category: Business & Finance
Title: Bootstrapping & VC Stories
Media Outlet: major national magazine
Specific Geographic Region: N
Region: USA

Deadline: 12:06pm EASTERN—05 June
Query:

I'm looking for:

1. Companies currently making the rounds trying to get VC funding, who are willing to talk about the experience. To qualify, you have to be getting in the door to pitch, although you don't actually have to be funded yet.

2. Successful startups that have bootstrapped rather than raising angel or VC investment. Here, I'm looking most likely for companies 1–3 years old, with at least a few million in annual revenue.

We want to learn how you launch and grow a startup in an era where capital and credit are so tight.

This is for a major US magazine. It's freelance, but I've been talking with an editor about it for a while.

HARO could be the gateway to getting your name and business in the media. Give it a go—after all, it's free.

In fact, I used the site when writing this book to consolidate some of my ideas and gain insights into how other freesourcers used their own dynamics to create their business. I received 85 replies from people willing to help and some of those ideas are hidden away in these pages. I will always credit people who have helped me out of courtesy and also to ensure that should we need to do business again, they are happy to impart their trusted knowledge to me.

Fee for a researcher helping to collate facts and figures for a magazine article: **£175**.

Obtain testimonials

If you are approaching someone to do business with, you need a compelling story to tell them. In any business environment, people like to do business with people they like. In most cases when starting a business from scratch you may not have a backstory or a trail of successes that the customer can look back on to make a decision on the risk involved in doing business with you. The more you can do to increase the likelihood of success with a new client, the better.

Let's start with you. Who are you and why should I do business with you? Answer this question well and you have overcome one barrier. But why not pre-empt the question and remove it earlier in the sales cycle to let you get on with the other processes involved in selling.

The way to do this is to get personal and professional testimonials in place and use them as you would a resumé, to inform the customer that you and your brand are credible and trustworthy to do business with.

With freesourcing this is easy. Get family, friends, colleagues, social networking sites and club members to do it for you. Just ask them for two or three sentences about who you are, what you did for them and why other people should do business with you.

A good example of this is the quotes that get used on the front of a book. If you see Peter Jones from *Dragons' Den* on the front saying "this is a great book," by association you will also think it's a great book. As an exercise for this book I went onto LinkedIn and asked my entire network to recommend me on the site—and I have to say I was overwhelmingly flattered. You can go and see the recommendations for yourself if you like—www.linkedin.com/in/jonathanyatesdotbiz.

Get your recommendations in order, and create a business-to-business CV about yourself and your business, including how long you have been in business, who your clients are, what your clients say about you and your work. Make your business credible to ensure that customers want to do business with you and don't give them any reason to say no when you approach them.

 Office space rental for a year: **£7000**.

Read trade magazines

Answer the following question: You want to start a business in an industry that:

1. You know everything about because you have been working in it for the last 30 years and no one can teach you anything because you wrote a book on the subject and it's published and everything.
2. You know nothing about. You just had a good idea and need to get it going, but are a little intimidated by the vast array of unknown words and phrases these people use.

Good news—it really doesn't matter if you answered 1 or 2, both answers are acceptable.

But in reality, you're unlikely to have answered 1 if you're reading this book (although you may have wanted an option in between). So how do you find out about your chosen industry? Trade journals are written by professional journalists with a history in the industry, whose job it is to find new methods to attract growth in readership and therefore bolster advertising revenue. These publications are in circulation for a reason: because they make money from advertisers by providing up-to-date information to their readership.

They are highly targeted. *Functional Food and Nutrition* is a cracking read for anyone involved with vitamins, minerals, food technology and nutrition, but for the pigeon breeder it's not such an important monthly read. *Dairy Innovation* is again brilliant for the food technologist, but just a little out of touch with dance teachers.

The best thing about these publications is that they use language you can only find in the industry. All those quirky technical words and abbreviations—the TLAs or three letter acronyms—the industries love them because it makes them sound as if they have specialist technical knowledge that outsiders can only marvel at. Lawyers and solicitors use legal speak, doctors and nurses (and gardeners) speak Latin and some builders speak *Eastenders*. If you're in the industry, it's important to learn this specialist language so that you're part of the club.

Once you've subscribed for free and it's delivered to your desk every month, your chosen trade journals will not only help you understand the language of your industry, they will also serve as great sources of supplier information, coming exhibitions, customer information and sales opportunities to the end of time.

If you did answer 1 to the question above, remember that you can always learn something new and put it to good use. Why don't you put finger to keyboard and write an article for a trade magazine to gain some extra networking and PR points?

Go out right now and borrow a magazine on a subject you know nothing about. It has to be interesting to someone for a reason. Even *Tunnels and Tunnelling International* magazine, which by the way will only set you back £99 a year should you subscribe, has a broad and diverse readership.

My advice is to get the paid-for magazines for free where possible. Phone up the publishers for a few previous copies to give you some background. They will usually send you one in the post in the hope that you will subscribe. I did this with one trade magazine and they still have me on the database, so it's been sent to me every month for the last four years. Some magazines are perfectly happy to supply you for free if you meet certain criteria—like being a senior manager or business owner in the industry—so it's worth checking.

Annual subscription to a research database and industrial news website: **£500.**

Benefit from an army of sales people

Do you want to spend time in your business or on your business? By *in* your business I mean doing those day-to-day things that move the business forward and produce cash flow. Working *on* the business is when you craft and mould it to produce a better and more efficient organization. For success in your chosen industry you need to do both: create a successful entity and push it forward.

The best place to be is getting the business going and leaving the sales to professionals. What better way to get a product moving than to pay people to sell some of your products? Sales agents and commission-only salespeople thrive on selling innovative products to their established network. You make a smaller amount per sale, but ultimately you shift more kit, more products or more service hours.

When you sell a product to an agent this works the same way as when you buy stock. Start with a sample case of the product for free or even a big discount to get them going; when they have successfully sold the initial case, they can use the profits to buy the next case and so on. As the business increases so will their customer base and repeat orders will start coming in.

The agent gets a value price for the product and you get the beginnings of a distribution network, which could grow organically into a network of distributors advertising your product by word of mouth and increasing the likelihood of repeat orders. And you haven't spent a thing.

A talented salesman took his first job as a commission-only computer hardware salesman just when the IT revolution was getting into full swing. He was very good at his job and made a lot of money selling to a growing set of clients. Very soon the company realized this and moved him into a better role, where he was selling just the microprocessors needed to run computers. His role was to manage sales to computer hardware manufacturers.

As part of his role he had to find new clients, not only sell to existing clients, and this he did. He found just six clients to whom he sold the microchips. After eight months of very hard work he had a new customer base.

One day the salesman realized that as he had found the six clients, he knew where the microprocessors were coming from and he was being paid commission only, he could cut out the company, set up on his own and take all the profits for himself. This is exactly what he did: he took his clients, set up on his own and carried on doing exactly the same thing, except this time instead of being paid commission, he was building his own company, hiring more staff and getting bigger orders. The company was sold and he retired very young to enjoy the fruits of his hard work.

Many large companies concentrate their own efforts on their core business and use a network of sales agents to ensure that non-traditional areas of their customer base are covered by people just like you. Get hold of a copy of *AgentBase* magazine and check out some of the adverts at www.sales-agents.com.

Many companies who use sales agents also want to ensure they provide the best training on the products or services those agents are representing in the field. You must remember this if you sign up sales agents for your organization: they are the ambassadors of your brand, engaging with your customer base and selling on your behalf. Make sure they are qualified to represent you by providing quality documentation and training materials.

Once you have an established a growing network of high-performing sales agents, introduce new and complementary products to augment the opportunity for both customers and agents. Most agents specialize in a specific market and therefore have good knowledge and contacts. Encourage them to sell your product alongside their existing offerings and ask them what else might sell to the same customers. This could be the beginnings of a great business for you and your sales agents.

Or you may decide that the commission-only route is better for you. Here are a few websites that specialize in the search for and recruitment of commission-only sales people:

→ Elance (http://www.elance.com)
→ PeoplePerHour.com (http://www.peopleperhour.com)
→ AgentBase (http://agentbase.com)
→ studentgems.com (http://www.studentgems.com)

There are legal implications of employing commission-only sales people—namely that if you make them redundant they can claim back lost commissions far into the future—so make sure you draw up a suitable contract and have it checked for free by a professional. There are many free and public domain contracts available online that you can tweak to your needs.

freeq One good-quality employed sales person: salary including commission, **£75,000**.

Get accredited

In order to give yourself some authority in the work you intend to carry out, it may be necessary to gain professional accreditation. Accreditation, together with your growing testimonials, gives new and potential customers a real feeling of confidence in your capabilities. To gain accreditation you need to join a professional body that represents businesses in your industry. The professional body will let you use its widely recognized logo on your marketing material.

However, many professional institutes charge a membership fee, which unfortunately does not help the freesourcing cause. They justify the fee as they provide bolt-on services such as access to a like-minded network of individuals in the same industry or discounted entry to exhibitions. They do offer industry-specific seminars and lectures aimed at keeping your knowledge and skills in this area of business up to date, and usually a monthly or quarterly magazine providing industry trends and analysis that will be invaluable for you to spot opportunities with.

So all in all it is a good idea to join a professional organization based around your industry and personal business needs, as you are then able to bolster your brand with the strength of a professional body. Most professional institutes let you add letters after your name as a bonus:

→ Member of the Chartered Institute of Marketing— MCIM
→ Fellow of the Royal College of Surgeons—FRCS
→ Chartered Institute of Management Accountants— CIMA
→ Chartered Management Institute—CMI
→ Professional Institute for Pipeline Engineers—PIPE
→ Chartered Institute of Building—CIOB

Think of it like an extra tag on your business card that shows which club you are in to prove your professional pedigree.

In order to get access to this club for free, ask for a trial period to see how it works for you. Many chartered institutes offer this service to see if you like them and they like you. During the trial period you are able to attend events but you're not a member, so you can't take advantage of the privileges this allows in terms of networking, research and information.

If you are unable to find free access to a group of like-minded individuals, then why not start your own local institute? I have just started the Institute of Freesourcing Practitioners (IoFP), of which I am a founder member, regular lecturer and contributor. If you would like to become a member for free, visit http://freesources.co.uk and sign in—you will then have the right, after signing our ethics policy and code of practice, to use the letters MIoFP on your marketing materials as well as after your name.

 Annual fee for first year's membership of the Professional Speakers' Association (including joining fee): **£250**.

Attend exhibitions

Exhibitions are fantastic free resources for entrepreneurs. Every industry has its associated exhibitions—from ball-bearing manufacturers to balloon specialists, there will be an exhibition. Whatever industry you wish to start a business in, one of the very first things you should do is visit an exhibition that relates to your product or service.

The opportunities are massive here: you have access to companies creating complementary products, to competitive research, to supplier resources, to free product giveaways, to networking, to industry-specific seminars, to sales opportunities. Visit www.exhibitions.co.uk to find one relevant for you.

Entry to an exhibition as a visitor is free nine times out of ten, because the organizers make their money from people buying stand space to promote their products and services. Exhibition organizers need people through the doors in the same way as magazine editors need a readership. The exhibitors have paid a fortune to be on a stand and they expect people to come and talk to them and discuss opportunities and make contacts, so you get into the exhibition for free.

There is a bonus here: if you are at an exhibition this gives you a certain amount of credibility without even having done any business. You automatically have something in common with everyone else in the industry because you attended the exhibition. Use this to leverage contacts and sales opportunities after the event. Go through all the business cards you collected and call them as soon as possible.

Hi Jim, it's Steve Mosely from Cardboard Cutouts. I saw you at Cardex 2010 and we spoke about your need for a new personalized freestanding cutout of your new

*product. Did you have a great show? I thought it could
have been better, I think last year was more productive
and next year if you use our cutout displays then it could
be more productive for you.*

In this example Steve might not even have attended the
event but merely asked the organizers for a list of exhibitors,
under the assumption that he is thinking of exhibiting next
year and wants to see the quality of the turnout. He may
have only been in business for a day, but talks about last
year and next year as if it was something he has been doing
for a lifetime.

But don't tell fibs, because you will get caught out and there
goes your credibility—use all situations to your advantage
and build credibility by references. People like to talk about
their own industries, so let them.

Check these websites for exhibitions in your chosen field:

→ Business Design Centre (www.businessdesigncentre.
   co.uk)
→ NEC Group (www.necgroup.co.uk)
→ SECC (www.secc.co.uk)
→ EC&O Venues (www.eco.co.uk)
→ Exhibitions.co.uk

Why not ask an organization that's taking a stand if you can
put your complementary products next to its display? If it
helps them get more people onto the stand, it will help you
by association—look for win/win situations.

When I was starting up I needed to get my product in front of an audience quickly, not only to advertise, but also to do some extensive research and taste testing and sell some product along the way. As I had very little cash, I approached the organizers of the Vitality Show in Scotland and asked if I could be a speaker on their lifestyle platform, one of four speaker areas within the exhibition. I have always been good at business presentations in front of audiences of up to 50 people, but this was different. We negotiated and I was given a substantial discount for the stand and the opportunity to speak to an audience.

Although a little nervous, I went ahead and every day for the four days of the show, I delivered a 40-minute presentation of my top 10 tips for business to audiences ranging between 20 and 200 people. Since this time, every time I do an exhibition I ask for a speaker slot. I don't charge a fee, instead I ask for a free stand. They need speakers and I need a stand. Deal done.

Exhibition stand 2m × 3m for a four-day event in London: **£3500**.

Get paid in advance

Cash flow can be a long and complex subject and you don't want to get yourself mixed up in difficult spreadsheets and financial reports, you just want to start your business for free. But you still need adequate cash flow.

To get paid in advance of doing a piece of work, you need a solid set of referrals and a credible work history that you have created on the way through this book. You have to create an environment of trust in your sales pitch so that when the time comes to ask, the client does not have a reason to say no to your request. So here is the trick:

To get paid for a job before you start, just ask for money up front.

It isn't in fact uncommon to get paid in advance. A really good example is the humble author. Authors get paid an advance to finish the book manuscript they have been sweating over and crafting for months on end, putting everything on hold until their latest blockbuster is ready. This advance—usually in two parts, an up-front payment and the final instalment on the delivery of the manuscript—acts as an incentive to finish the book and deliver the work to the publisher on time, while enabling the author to concentrate on writing the book rather than worrying about where the next meal is coming from. This system works well for both the publisher and the author, as it keeps everyone's minds keenly focused on the task at hand.

After starting up my own business and then selling it, I wondered what I could do next. What I now had in my collection of experiences was a successful track record in the field of entrepreneurship. I was always struck by how impressed people were with the story of a back-bedroom start-up moving through all the stages of building a business up to a trade sale. Once the information had got out, people asked me if I would come to their events and speak about my experiences and share what I'd done right and wrong along the way.

After 10 or so free appearances, I decided to start charging for my services as a professional speaker. All I had to do to command a four-figure amount for an hour's work was to tell my story in a style that fitted the event. I used the first income from this to buy books on public speaking and joined Toastmasters and the Professional Speakers' Association. I did this because as a paid speaker I needed to become better at my new craft and provide tailored presentations and speeches that would help my credibility and reputation grow. I now speak in public at least once a week and enjoy expanding my network and getting to know new and diverse industries.

Many other businesses get paid in advance. A good example is IT. If the technology a customer believes it needs is not commercially available, the customer might invest in a technology at a very early stage in the product development lifecycle. They may buy an exclusive alpha release at a discounted price to enable the IT firm to build on the platform with a real-world customer and start delivering quick benefits while finishing off the development of the product.

There are hundreds (if not thousands) of small software houses on the web that only ask for a donation to keep their software development dreams alive. They use PayPal to take small payments from happy customers who would like to see the software developed further. For example, Hootsuite (http://hootsuite.com) provides its Twitter-related software and support for free, including development and new releases, just asking for a simple donation in return. If you use the site for free and it helps you in your business, then why not say thank-you in a way that will help the developer?

To get paid in advance, negotiate to get the deal you want. Don't merely ask for half the money up front, give your reasons. Create a believable story to get the customer on your side:

→ I need the money up front because I need to buy the raw materials in order to make the treehouse. It's built to order, so I am having to take the risk early on.
→ We are in a downturn and it would really help if we could get paid in advance. I'll even give you a 10% discount if you could confirm early.
→ You need to book me in advance and pay a deposit because my time is my job and I need to manage my calendar effectively.
→ I need to develop the next stage of the software before I can release the new improved version to the user base.

Cash is king, so make sure you offer the right reasons and offer an incentive. This can work for all levels of business (and it regularly does). In order to bring other early payments into your business, why not offer alternative methods of payment: credit card, personal cheque with a guarantee card, cash—it's all money in the end, you just need to give your customers the option.

 No Freeq here as cash is king.

This chapter has been about creating a brand, an identity and a customer base and managing them. I would like to end the chapter with some golden rules of selling:

1. Find out what the customer needs before you sell them what you have.
2. Good rapport is vital to the sales process. Engage the prospect first.
3. No two sales are the same, so adapt your presentation to the customer's requirements.
4. When people say no, ask why not. Address each barrier with a competent answer and ask again for the sale.
5. Never drop your price. Negotiate discounts for delivery, extra components or services, but keep the core price the same.
6. Sales do not stop at the financial transaction, excellent customer service must follow.

Sales is just a conversation about your business. If you have everything sorted at the outset—the right brand, the right product, the right place to do business at the right time with the right customer and at the right price—there is no reason anyone should say no. This is the case for the largest IT contract and for selling ice creams on a sunny day. Get everything right and the sales will come. Sales only become difficult when you haven't worked on your business enough.

Total Freeq Value

Circa **£156,000**

7

Growth and Next Steps

Now your business is trading and you are making money, you need to congratulate yourself. Look back on the work you've done to get to this point and start to plan your next steps.

At this juncture you have a few choices to make. You may just want to carry on the business and enjoy being your own boss, making enough to put away some pennies and go on the odd holiday every year. It may be that you would like to grow the business into a 10-person venture, so that you can retire early and let someone else run the business while you spend your days enjoying the luxuries in life while attending a few board meetings here and there. Or you could take the plunge and go for the big one: grow the business to the point of a trade sale, cash in all your hard work and go and live on a magical island somewhere. Of course, this all depends on the type of business and your own capabilities and ultimate desires. If you do want to grow the business into something more than a sole trader, read on.

The great feature you possess is the hard fact that you have started a business and you have managed to do this by minimizing resources and maximizing profits. Whether you have made a great deal of money or not, you are already an attractive investment opportunity both as a business and, more importantly, as a person who can start and run a business.

When looking at investments, venture capitalists, business angels and banks look for a track record. They see hundreds of presentations, business plans and executive summaries from people who have had an idea but have yet to start a business in any shape or form. These start-ups are looking for seed capital, money to help them get going. They are risky for investors as they have no track record. You, on the other hand, have a track record, a proven idea and a growing customer base. You can make projections on income and have little or no requirement for seed capital. What you now need is growth capital, which is a much more powerful proposition.

Remember everything you have learned so far. As it grows, your business may get bloated with sales and fat on profits, which can make it sluggish. Don't have a business coronary. Trim some of the fat and focus on healthy habits to ensure the business is lean and fighting fit. You always need to think like an entrepreneur, maintaining cost control and looking for free inputs. Resist the desire to spend money and try the alternatives first.

It is interesting to note the well-known statistic that 80% of millionaires drive second-hand cars! Millionaires got to where they are today because they know where they can save money without having to sacrifice quality.

Forms of growth capital

So you need money to grow and there are other people who have money to invest. Who are they? Where are they? How do you get them investing in you?

Investors will buy into a business for a number of reasons:

→ They want the technology it possesses.
→ They want the business before the competition gets it.
→ They are too lazy to develop a competitive product or service and to enter a market that they can see has possibilities.
→ They see that you are the value in the company and they want you to help them make money.

This last one is the key: investors buy into you and then they buy into your business.

The main sources of growth capital are discussed briefly below.

Business angels

Business Angels provide startup capital for new businesses. They are often wealthy individuals or consortiums who enjoy lending money to new ventures in return for a share in the business. An increasing number of angel investors organize themselves into angel networks, so they can share research and pool their investment capital to invest in larger opportunities. This can be fantastic for a start-up in need of a panel of mentors with a range of specific skills. Search for a local group of angels at the British Business Angels Association, http://bbaa.org.uk.

Venture capitalists

Venture capital is provided by organizations looking to profit from early stage innovation. Like Business Angels, a venture capitalist might lend a new startup cash in return for shares in the company or a long term convertible loan. Venture capitalists specialise in generating profit from new business innovations so have a keen eye for opportunity and a robust selection and decision making process.

However, venture capital is not easy to obtain, as this quote from venture capitalist Guy Kawasaki illustrates:

Someone once told me that the probability of an entrepreneur getting venture capital is the same as getting struck by lightning while standing at the bottom of a swimming pool on a sunny day. This may be too optimistic.

If you're feeling brave and you think your company fits the profile, contact the British Venture Capital Association (www.bvca.co.uk).

Banks

Simply put, banks are large buildings full of other people's money. The banks make a return on the money you lend to them for safe keeping by investing in stock markets, commodities, businesses and loans, among other things. In recent years banks have made some terrible investment decisions and since the financial crisis, the criteria for assessing the risk of lending your business money have become extremely detailed. As comedian Bob Hope put it:

A bank is a place that will lend you money if you can prove that you don't need it.

Government

The UK government loves small business start-ups. Entrepreneurs create jobs and push the boundaries of innovation. It is the role of the government and the Department for Business, Innovation and Skills (www.berr.gov.uk) to actively encourage the growth of your business.

If you think government help would benefit your business, have a look on the j4b grants database (www.j4b.co.uk), which lists over 4500 different grants and incentives. Someone has to be given these grants, why shouldn't it be you?

Some inspiration

I thought I would finish with a couple of stories that encompass all the tenets in the book. The first was provided by

Deirdre Bounds, creator of i-to-i, the world's largest gap-year travel company, and the second by Alex Bellinger, creator and editor of SmallBizPod, the UK's most popular podcast dedicated to small businesses and entrepreneurs.

---

i-to-i

i-to-i may have started in a bedsit in Leeds, but the idea was a culmination of four years' travelling and teaching abroad. After she returned to Leeds from her travels, Deirdre became a youth worker and a stand-up comic. Both careers were to become very useful to her business. Her time spent as a youth worker gave her access to young people who could only dream of taking a gap year. The problem became apparent that there were no affordable ways to take a safe gap year. Once you see the problem, coming up with a solution is easy. Deirdre saw the need to change gap years from only being available in the charitable sector to being made available in the travel sector, which instantly widened the market. i-to-i became a tour operator.

To begin with she needed cash, so to "bootstrap" she started to train young people how to teach English as a foreign language, tailored her offering for sixth formers in the Leeds area and with her youth work connections managed to sell this into 14 schools. Deirdre then branched out into weekend courses. All payments were requested in advance, so there were no cash-flow issues.

i-to-i grew from nothing because Deirdre became an expert in the art of barter. A local university created the artwork for her company as part of a £50 competition. Her first offices were in a sixth form college in exchange for two i-to-i courses. She sponsored travel shows and student events, offering courses and trips as prizes, and then went on TV programme *Wife Swap* to get i-to-i in front of six million viewers for free.

So where did the stand-up comedy training come in useful? When Deirdre was booed off stage by 300 people in a Nottingham nightclub and cried all the way back to Leeds, she vowed then and there that nothing could be as humiliating as that experience—funnily enough, it never was. That night she conquered her fear of failure: when you reach rock bottom you can only look up. Bedsit to sale to a FTSE 100 for an eight-figure sum in 11 years. Find out more at www.deirdrebounds.com.

SmallBizPod

For Alex Billinger, SmallBizPod was an accidental business waiting to happen when he launched it back in March 2005. He didn't expect it to become his first real start-up, but it's now the UK's most popular podcast dedicated to small businesses and entrepreneurs in Apple's iTunes charts.

The beauty of the Internet is that you can experiment quickly, make mistakes, iterate an idea and get customer feedback for virtually no money at all. In fact, SmallBizPod was started for *literally* no money at all. Other than a computer Alex already had and an old microphone from a kid's karaoke set, everything he needed to record, edit, distribute and promote SmallBizPod was online and free.

He created a Blogger account (www.blogger.com) and set up a blog site for the podcasts, used Skype to call interviewees, Audacity to record and edit, Feedburner to create and track the Internet feed that automated downloads, podcast directories and review sites for publicity and distribution, and finally Apple's podcasting section of iTunes when it launched later in 2005.

After about 12 months the podcast really started to get traction, with listener numbers increasing rapidly and mainstream media coverage helping to raise its profile too. Alex then started getting calls from large brands interested in sponsorship. It dawned on him that SmallBizPod could be the real business idea he'd been looking for. Other than his own time, he'd created an opportunity from nothing and he realized that people were willing to pay him for something he was passionate about. A business was born. Explore SmallBizPod for yourself at www.smallbizpod.co.uk.

Conclusion

The contents of this book make starting a business for free sound easy at face value. But turning an idea into a business is not an easy task, however much money you have. Hopefully this book and the ideas described within it will have gone some way in preparing you for the road ahead and, more than that, will have enabled you to think like an entrepreneur from the start by asking yourself two questions: "How can I do it cheaper? How can I do it better?"

There are a vast number of businesses that can be started for free. Throughout the book I have outlined the steps and thoughts that you need to undertake in order to start a business with your specific idea and experience. Choose the relevant track and go for it.

Open your eyes and watch how others have taken up the freesourcing challenge. Most freesource start-up businesses are based around two fundamental assets: a service you can provide and your time. You may be giving your services for free at the moment for selfless motives. Why not start charging or bartering with these services to start out on your own?

Thank you for reading this book. I really hope you have learned a great deal and that you're encouraged by the fact that you do not need megabucks to start a successful business. What it really takes is hard work—lots of hard work with a bit of extra hard work thrown in.

Now it's up to you to develop your business and decide what your next steps are. For many the next step is to expand by buying more stock, employing more people and investing more in the business. I am right behind you all the way and look forward to hearing about the success of your Freestart.

One final thought to end this chapter on growth and next steps. When you look back on how you started your business, keep in mind the advice and options in this book. Don't splash out the cash, conserve your money and look for value alternatives or even free alternatives. Just because your business is a larger entity doesn't mean you should fall back on habits that will suck the cash reserves dry. Once a freesourcer, always a freesourcer. Good luck and let me know the outcome.

Freestarts: More Businesses You Can Start for Free

There have been examples of Freestarts throughout the book—here are a few more to give you inspiration.

Artist

Creating art for pleasure and then turning a profit from it might be the greatest gift of all. You can start by collecting seashells and flotsam and jetsam from the beach, twigs and flowers from the woods, metal from the tip or anything else you can lay your hands on. Create magical works linked to your location that you can sell on to tourists looking for a personalized and unique memento of their holiday. Get into the local paper by sending in a picture of your creations and explaining why you started the business when a holiday maker approached you while you were creating a masterpiece and asked to buy it. Approach hotels and ask them to exhibit paintings and creations for you. When a purchaser buys your work, share the profits with the hotel. When the hotel and you have a good rapport, suggest that you both might make a bit extra by placing items in every room with a for sale sign on them. If you are worried about the towel stealers, then at the very least put in a card with a picture on it. When you start supplying one hotel, approach a larger chain and use your experience to sell the idea into a bigger audience.

 ## Author/writer

Get a free computer from Freecycle, load the Ubuntu operating system onto it and add the necessary writing, email and Internet tools. A free online wordprocessor, data storage for back-up and sharing technology are available from http://docs.google.com (this is what I am using right now!). Write a good, well-thought-out and relevant book with a specific target market in mind. Upload your work to sell at a good price through websites such as Lulu (www.lulu.com), Bookhabit (www.bookhabit.com) and ClickBank (www.clickbank.com). Earn enough money to self-publish your book with Lulu or WritersWorld (www.writersworld.co.uk). Send a hard copy of the book with a letter and sales info to WHSmith, Borders, Waterstones and other book-store chains and get them to say they would stock the book if you find a publisher. Ask them to recommend a publisher and commissioning editor. Send the book, a letter, testimonials and a biography to your new contact. Get a publishing contract. Write your second, third and fourth books (this is exactly what I did with my first book, *All-time Essentials for Entrepreneurs*).

 ## Babysitter

Who wouldn't want to spend a quiet Saturday night in watching a DVD and eating some nice food curled up on the sofa, especially when it is someone else's house and you are getting paid to be there? Create some flyers, print them out on your Freecycle printer and post them to neighbours in the local area. Get some advice on babysitting from the Internet and become an expert. Be professional and arrange a mutually beneficial date on your own time to introduce yourself to the family before the date. Make friends with the children so they know who you are. Create a website for people to book and use a special password given out to those families who use the service. If you are unable to fulfil a time they book, arrange for a trusted friend to fill in on your behalf and split the profits with them. Grow the business by getting a reputation as the best in the area and train up your own babysitting associates who can be booked out over your website. Get CRB (Criminal Records Bureau) checked in advance as it's a requirement for this business that you're seen as a responsible adult to whom parents can entrust their children; and if you do use other people to work with you, get them checked as well.

 ## Bookkeeper

With more and more people starting out on their own, bookkeeping skills are in great demand. Any business needs a basic accounting system and to be able to report on how money is flowing through the business. There are free online courses as well as practical help from Business Link in the UK to help you develop your skills in this essential area of business. A single bookkeeper can command a good hourly rate of pay and handle 20 clients comfortably from their own home. It is an essential skill in business which many startups lack, to be able to manage finances at their most basic level. Approach friends and family for contacts, create business cards with credible references and use networking events to grow your business.

Car registration broker

Set yourself up as a car registration broker to sell personalized number plates. Set up a database (often taken from the national newspapers and car magazines) of companies that have stocks of number plates. When you receive an enquiry from a possible customer, find the dealer with that registration if it is available, buy the number plate from the dealer and sell it to the customer. You have brokered the deal and got the cash up front before paying the wholesaler. You could also check out the DVLA website (www.dvla.gov.

uk), learn how to create custom number plates for your customers and carry out the registration process for them.

Car valeting

Valeting is more than just a car wash, it's a loving and caring car beautician service. Offer your services to people in the local area who don't have the time or the inclination to wash their own cars. Offer to wash the car at work or perhaps during a shopping trip, so they can get on with one thing while you get their car looking brand new. Differentiate your offering with excellent customer service and attention to detail. Set up a monthly standing order service for your regular clients, say £15.00 for a bronze service, £25 for a silver service and £50 for a gold service.

→ Bronze—up to two washes with a wax shine, interior hoover and tidy per month.
→ Silver—up to thee washes with a wax shine, interior hoover and tidy per month—anywhere.
→ Gold—weekly full service on any day with special weekend buff-up service.

This guarantees your income and ensures cash flow. Like a gym membership, not everyone will want the service all of the time. Put the hard work into this business to make it look like a professional and branded service, which you might then think about franchising round the country using a website for customers to book its services centrally. Theme your car wash team's uniforms with national holidays and the season to create a buzz about the service.

Children's party entertainer

freestart

Can you entertain a group of rowdy 6–8 year olds? Parents struggle to find the next party venue or clown for a children's party. Make it easy and provide a complete service for them. Asking for half the money up front will ensure no unnecessary worries about venue fees and food requirements. Think of a character that you can play and visit second-hand shops to find a costume. Practice your 30-minute set on your own children and their friends. Liaise with local village halls and play centres to get the best rate to keep costs down and profits high. Learn skills that children can appreciate: a little magic and juggling might be a good starter. Offer to provide party bags for the children with presents and the cake. Take all the worry off the parents by sitting down and getting to know the child at a prebooked meeting. Find out what they want and then create a whizz bang party that their friends will be talking about at school the next Monday morning. You could always offer your services to local schools on special event days such as fêtes, fairs and sports days, where some of the children's brothers and sisters might be attending and need to be looked after. Get CRB (Criminal Records Bureau) checked in advance as it's a requirement for this business that you're seen as a responsible adult to whom parents can entrust their children.

DIY expert

freestart

Give someone the gift of time by offering to do those jobs around the house that they've put to one side for the past six months. Putting up shelves, laying the new carpet, washing the windows, recovering chairs, painting the outside furniture, rewaxing the work surfaces, sanding the floors, hanging the picture, moving the cupboards—you get the idea (and this is just my list!). Borrow the tools from the home owner or from your network to get the jobs done. Be professional and create a work list with the customer in advance, sit down with them and talk through what needs to be done. Inspect the property with them and suggest things that you might be able to do as an extra revenue stream. Turn up on the day and work the hours you agreed at the price you agreed. Make sure that each job is signed off and give the customer a questionnaire at the end to ask if they were happy with the work and for them to provide a sentence or two for the website you are putting together. When you can, get some fridge magnets made up and leave one with your happy customer as a reminder next time they, or any of their friends, need some help. Happy customers talk about your service, as do unhappy ones. For larger jobs and contractual work, ask friends to come and help you out and share the profits.

Dog walker/dog grooming services

You have to love our canine friends for this one. Walking five dogs at a time (and clearing up after them) is a business on the rise. People are very time poor at the moment as they work hard to maintain their existing lifestyles. If you can help then claw back some of this time by helping out, they will pay you handsomely for it. Collect the dogs, take them for a walk, clean up after them then, using the money you have made to buy some dog-washing kit, special brushes, shampoo and so on and extend the business. You can also sell dog owners bulk delivery of dog chow, special dog water, bedding, dog beds and playtime accessories. You would be barking to give this one a miss.

 ## Domestic cleaner/housekeeper/ ironing

Service industries are growing faster than any other section of the start-up business community. People are working harder and longer hours and just don't get the time to do household chores, the shopping or the garden. Offer your services for £10 per hour for you to complete a list of household chores. If you can retain just 5 clients a week for 2 hours a day, that's an extra £100 a week. This means that your clients will have to work harder to come up with your fee, which leaves them even less time to do the chores and therefore generates more opportunities for you to help them out at home. Excellent!

 ## Fitness instructor

Fitness and wellbeing may be your hobby, so get fit and show other people how to get fit in a planned, set programme. Start an outdoor fitness club in the park using the benches, tree stumps and playground as a multipurpose gym. Devise exercise programmes and offer to teach them to people in their own homes. Be a paid jogging buddy to encourage people to keep going.

Foraging tutor

You may be a mycology and foraging enthusiast, always rooting around for mushrooms, herbs and leaves to spice up the family meal at home. Research your local area at the library or learn with an online group to expand the breadth of your knowledge and deep-down facts. At the weekend, encourage people in your network to come on walks with you looking for free foods in the woods and meadows, and explain how these can be used in everyday cooking. These trips could be charged at £5 each and with a group of 10 people this might be a good morning's work. When your business has grown to a respectable level, begin offering your services to local restaurants. On quiet days, a restaurant might let you work out of one of their kitchens. A foraging trip in the morning could then become a food preparation lesson in the afternoon using the ingredients you have gathered and enjoying a gourmet hand-picked lunch. The restaurant gets customers through the door on a quiet day, which becomes a regular event. You may well be able to expand the business to become a management training course for businesses looking for a different bonding session for their staff. Remember to get your clients to sign a liability waiver just in case the mushroom they pick turns out to be different to the one in your book.

Freesource consultant

Use your time and the knowledge you've gained from this book to show people how to start up a business for free! In a difficult economic climate people look for alternatives to their current employment and many want to start up a home-based business just to make ends meet. You might choose to run a series of low-cost seminars to show people how they could take advantage of all the free resources out there to start up successfully on their own. (See http://freesources.co.uk for more details on courses and seminars in your local area.)

freestart Gold harvesting

There are roughly 25 billion ounces of gold dissolved in the world's oceans and currently no economical way of extracting them. Find a way to extract gold dissolved in seawater. At current rates there are approximately 400 ounces of gold per cubic mile of seawater and gold is selling for around $900 per ounce. So for every cubic mile of seawater, you could extract $360,000 of revenue. Is this worth a few years' investment in finding a solution?

freestart Graphic design

Get your hands on a computer and transfer your design skills from the art room to the screen. Find a product or service that needs a design makeover. Do the makeover and do it extremely well. Find the contact in the business who is responsible for its overall design requirements and create a carefully crafted letter outlining why you think the design needs a change. I say carefully, as this person may have initiated the current design and may not take too kindly to your view that it is outdated, outmoded or not strong enough. Wait until the design and letter have been received and then call the person to introduce yourself as the origina-tor of the work and ask if you can come in to explain further why your design should be taken on board. This proactive approach shows your willingness to do business, which com-panies admire and cherish because it means you're not just another cold call. You've done the research and can see the whys and hows of the business. It's your job to convert this excellent foundation work into a sale; at this stage it shouldn't be too difficult. If you don't get the design contract, ask for a comment on the work and permission to use it in your portfolio for the next time you approach a business. Submit the design to reputable web forums for discussion of your work and magazines that might include it and its rationale in its pages. You need a portfolio of designs and success stories to encourage new clients to do business with you. Sell your designs on zazzle.com and istockphoto.com.

 ## Lawn sculptor

Do you like the outdoors whatever the weather? Take the lawnmower out of your garage and offer to mow people's gardens for a fee. How many times a year do you actually use the lawnmower? Six, seven, maybe ten at most. For about 350 days of the year your grass-cutting machinery is sitting idle. Put it to good use and, like all good plant and machinery, let it work for you. While it sits idle it's gathering dust and depreciating. Look at your neighbour's lawns (unless you're in an apartment) and suggest that you could cut the grass if they're too busy. Get more business by approaching schools and businesses with the service and offering to tend their plants as well. Grow the business by purchasing or hiring a hedge trimmer or getting one on Freecycle and do the hedges as well. Then think about providing lawn care maintenance services with regular visits, organic treatments for lawns and a customer care package.

 ## Local history tour guide

Spend some time at your local library brushing up on interesting facts and figures on the history of your own town and village. Meet tourists when they are dropped off at bus and train stations and offer them a one-hour tour of the area. Call local tour companies and ask them to include you on the list of activities they are offering to their customers. To get your speaking confidence to a competent level, attend Toastmasters International (www.toastmasters.org): the first few sessions are free and you can pick up a whole host of great tips and tricks from just sitting and listening to the experts. Ensure referrals by asking people who attend your tour to fill in a questionnaire that you can use to hone your tour experience and add to any marketing material to attract more business. Add a free listing to Yell.com and other Internet listing sites. Speak at events for free on your chosen topic to inform people in the local area of your service. Write a blog using the knowledge you have gained and link it to a sign-up form for enquiries.

Outside catering

Approach local businesses and events companies with a flyer that you have created yourself with the free computer and printer you have managed to freesource. Offer your services as a contract caterer and provide samples at the first meeting you have with the client. If necessary, offer to do the first gig at a lower cost in order to get your foot in the door and gain valuable testimonials. Ask the client for half the money up front in order that you can source the freshest and best ingredients for the function. Add specific details that you might become known by, such as a certain quality dish or a small food gift for each guest to take home. Be memorable. Make sure you check out the food and hygiene regulations at www.food.gov.uk.

 ## Personal stylist/shopper

Do you have an eye for a great bargain and do you know what the next hot fashion item is? Do you enjoy shopping using other people's money? If the answer to all of these is yes, then set yourself up in business as a fashion stylist, helping clients dress to impress. All this great business idea takes is word of mouth and a little creative advertising.

Photographer

Get your hands on a camera from Freecycle or borrow a camera from a friend, set up a website with contact details and register for a Flickr photo-sharing account (www. flickr.com). Take a really good picture of a celebrity/hotel/ product/building. Go to the manager of the celebrity/hotel/ product/building and say they can have the picture royalty free in return for a testimonial, recommendation or repeat business. Use the fact that you have supplied commercial photographic artwork for that celebrity/hotel/product/ building in your growing portfolio. Carry on building the business.

Professional speaker

Pick a topic you can speak confidently on, that has an identifiable audience and that is in demand. Create a biography and ask for testimonials from your network. Many professional speakers have a "hook" that makes them unique and therefore different to all other speakers. What is your hook and why is it different? Get some real live practice in with friends and family. Find some clients using freely available networking tools and events. Offer your first speaking events for free to schools, colleges and local venues. Commercialize your events by gaining a reputation as an expert in your chosen field. Businesses that want to add some sparkle to their corporate events are the ones to approach. Get in touch with local event organizers: they could be the key to your success by actively recommending you as part of their offering. Join professional speaker bureaus and don't be put off by some of the big names they have on their websites. You are creating a unique offering in the professional speaker world and so should be in demand. Join the Professional Speakers' Association (www. professionalspeakersassociation.co.uk) and Toastmasters International (www.toastmasters.org) to grow your skills and find new customers by referral from fellow speakers.

Recruiter

Finding someone a job can be one of the most satisfying and rewarding undertakings there is. Ask yourself what you need: basically a set of candidates and some jobs to fill. Find a job advert placed by a local company on

Monster (www.monster.co.uk) and search online for a suitable candidate in the area. Your expertise comes by supplying the right candidate for the job and ensuring that they
provide value to the company. Specialize in a specific area
and create your experience around this niche. Create a database of candidates and ask for candidates who have been
placed if they know of anyone else who might be able to fill
the role. This industry is extremely sales focused and you
need to make sure that you have expert networking skills
and read all you can on industry trends. Start out on your
own and then grow the business by recruiting associates
who are self-employed but use your premises and equipment and share the finder's fee 50/50. Grow this associate
model and run the business.

 ## Room rental

Rent out a room in your house to an exchange
student to earn extra money, understand what it means to
manage rental accommodation and use this expertise to
manage rentals for other clients. The industry standard for
rental service fees is between 9% and 15%. Offer a tailored
service and grow the business.

Secretarial services

To get small office jobs done, many companies
don't feel the need to incur the cost of an agency temp. Get
your hands on some office equipment cheaply from eBay or
our old friend Freecycle and offer local business and friends
much needed services like proofreading, audio typing, direct

mail campaign coordination, filing, simple accounts, arranging travel or appointment booking for conferences. To differentiate yourself from the market, charge on a per project basis so your customers can keep control of the costs and you can provide a professional service.

 ## Snorkelling/swimming tours

Do you yearn for the open water, the sea lapping at your ears, exploring the coastline of some warm-watered lagoon? You have the opportunity to create a business based on your hobby. Take people on tours of your favourite snorkelling sites. Take them abroad (get them to pay up front)—there is someone already doing this, by the way. Make sure you have the correct insurance and travel docs in place, otherwise make sure that all members of the group sign a disclaimer and have their own insurance.

Tipster

If you like the gee gees and a flutter but have no money, offer your knowledge of racing form as a top tipster. Get clients to call in for dead certs on the 2.15 at Newmarket and instead of them paying you, get them to put on 10% extra for you. That way you only get paid when they win with the tips you have provided. If you are successful your credibility goes through the roof, thus enabling you to grow the business by word of mouth. Ensure you study the form, because the success of this business depends on your skill in selecting the right horses. Create a website of your services and use careful predictions to update the site and make sure you include a disclaimer about people losing money as a result of your advice. Do not use your own money to bet.

 ## Tutor

Every parent wants the best for their precious little lambs and when they come home from school with a report that doesn't shine very brightly, worry sets in. I have settled on kids here but there is vast scope for tutoring adults as well. Offer your services as a subject tutor. If you have expertise in accountancy, then teach maths. If you have expertise in IT, teach computing. Why not act as a careers tutor, showing kids and parents what options they might pursue founded on their hobbies, interests and qualifications? This is working at the periphery of being a life coach, but helping someone find their role in society can be extremely important. You might even be able to start a business based around your skills as a study tutor who can teach children and adults the best and most constructive methods for learning. Many parents are out of touch with modern teaching methods and as such are unable to help their kids in the best way. Teach the parents how to help the children. Advertise by word of mouth and reputation. Update your knowledge on the subject and relearn out-of-date language and technical skills on the Internet. Download study plans and amend them for your audience. Try out new ways of teaching.

Walking coach

You like getting exercise, you like a nice walk. Find out how to walk correctly and most efficiently for fitness (yes, there is a method), then get people interested in learning what you know and take them out in groups according to their fitness levels. Walking is one of the healthiest forms of exercise there is and in difficult times not everyone wants to pay for gym membership. Walking keeps you fit—and the fitness industry is on the rise.

Web designer

Using a free computer and free tools to get on the Internet, design simple yet effective web pages. You could even start a business that helps people get a free computer and free tools to help them start a web business...

For more Freestarts and to submit your own Freestart ideas please visit www.freesources.co.uk

The 10 Rules of Freesourcing

In compiling this book and creating what is now commonly understood as freesourcing, certain truths have become apparent. The freesourcing ethic in its simplest form aims to help people understand that they do not require huge sums of start-up capital to get their business on the road. Instead, by adhering to simple steps, anyone with an idea can create and move a business forward with very little more than time and effort.

I created the 10 rules of freesourcing to ensure that the freesource movement understands the fundamentals of how to practise good freesourcing conduct, for the benefit of both themselves and others in the business community. These rules are not set in stone but are meant to act as best practice as more and more people take up the challenge of freesourcing. Stick to these rules and you won't go far wrong.

1. Freesourcers use what they have to get what they need.

2. Freesourcers never take more than they need.

3. Freesourcers value relationships more than money.

4. Freesourcers seek out creative alternatives.

5. Freesourcers see time as more valuable than money.

6. **Freesourcers learn about other people's businesses.**

7. **Freesourcers understand that free may not always mean best quality.**

8. **Freesourcers always give something back in return for what they take.**

9. **Freesourcers conjure brilliance from nothing.**

10. **Freesourcers start businesses for more than just money.**

To view the forums and get a more in-depth feel for the freesourcing rules and ethics, visit www.freesources.co.uk.

Glossary

FREE—Provided without, or not subject to, a charge or payment.

FREECONOMY—The common social system of production, exchange, distribution and consumption of the goods and services of a geographical area where no financial or monetary return is offered or exchanged.

FREECYCLE—The act of donating and receiving free goods and services using the Freecycle.org network.

FREEDOM—The result of a committed change of lifestyle to enjoy your own aspirations.

FREEGAN—People who employ alternative strategies for living based on limited participation in the conventional economy and minimal consumption of resources. Freegans embrace community, generosity, social concern, freedom, cooperation and sharing in opposition to a society based on materialism, moral apathy, competition, conformity and greed. (Definition taken from the http://freegan.org. uk website.)

FREEMIUM—A business model that works by offering basic services for free, while charging a premium for advanced or special features. The business model has gained popularity with the new wave of Internet companies who encourage trial and viral propagation of its services.

FREEQ—Or freesourcing equivalent, the cash value you would have spent on a good or service should you have paid for the item with traditional means. For example, the Freeq of a Freecycle-obtained PC with Ubuntu operating system might be the cash value of a similar Windows-based machine purchased online. Therefore the Freeq would be, say, £450.

FREESAUCE—Sachets of ketchup you might be able to use for free in a café or fish and chip restaurant (not to be confused with freesource).

FREESOURCE—A resource that a business is able to use for its benefit that has been found, borrowed or created for no initial monetary outlay.

FREESOURCER—An entrepreneur who has started and grown a business with no money apart from that which the company has generated, and people within business who is actively using the freesourcing ethic to create business growth. The size of the business is irrelevant as any sized organization can benefit from the ideology.

FREESOURCERY—The ability to find the ultimate freesources with apparent ease, a magical freesource touch.

FREESOURCING—The act of locating and using a freesource.

FREESOURCING EQUIVALENT—See Freeq.

FREESTART—A business you can start up for free.

FREETIME—Spare time left over from your normal day-to-day activities that is currently underused or inappropriately employed.

Acknowledgements

I would like to dedicate this book to JP, who once accused me of being tight. This was during a particular stormy night in a hotel bar in London where, as a very close group of friends, we were discussing what we least liked about each other's personalities. I would like to put the record straight and admit that he was probably right those many, many years ago and also take the chance to say thank you for pointing it out to me in front of everyone. If I was not careful with money in business then I would not have been able to create the business I have today or even have the basics with which to write this book on freesourcing.

So thank you JP, always a mine of wisdom. I would like to make recompense by offering you a drink at a bar of your choosing (in the UK) any time you like (as long as it's happy hour) and the round comes to no more than £3.50 for two drinks. Can't say fairer than that, cobber. At least being tight is marginally better than having a performance car.

Jonathan Yates, at the kitchen table, Harrogate, November 2009

About the Author

When inspiration, dedication and motivation meet head on, great things happen to people. When they met in the head of Jonathan Yates, they created a maverick entrepreneur who would go on to win awards, praise and accolades for his skill at grasping the concept of successful business.

Jonathan founded his own business, Santeau, in his back bedroom and sold the business four years later. Through dogged tenacity and unshakable self-belief, he has appeared in the national press and international radio on countless occasions, once having his top ten tips for business success compared to those of business mogul and chairman of TV show *The Apprentice* Lord Sugar. In the *Sunday Times*, businessman and *Dragons' Den* stalwart Peter Jones praised Jonathan for his business instinct, saying "It won't be long before he gets a loyal following."

Jonathan has motivated many entrepreneurs into action with his regular seminars and professional speaking events. Using proven techniques and expertise, he shows people how and when to make the necessary adjustments to achieve their goals, and how to capture and control inspiration, dedication and motivation.

Jonathan is also the author of *All-Time Essentials for Entrepreneurs* (Capstone), a miscellany of essential facts, tips and advice that every entrepreneur needs to know to be successful. Written in the knowledge that entrepreneurs have to find valuable information quickly, the book harnesses the energy and inspiration of several books and provides the instant gratification that appeals to this market.

Jonathan is 40 and lives in Harrogate, North Yorkshire with his wife Lisa and their three boys, Harry, Fred and Patrick.